MW01225589

Zend Studio™
for Eclipse

Developer's Guide

Peter MacIntyre
Ian Morse

Pearson Education, 800 East 96th Street, Indianapolis, Indiana 46240 USA

Zend Studio™ for Eclipse Developer's Guide

Copyright © 2008 by Pearson Education, Inc.

All rights reserved. No part of this book shall be reproduced, stored in a retrieval system, or transmitted by any means, electronic, mechanical, photocopying, recording, or otherwise, without written permission from the publisher. No patent liability is assumed with respect to the use of the information contained herein. Although every precaution has been taken in the preparation of this book, the publisher and authors assume no responsibility for errors or omissions. Nor is any liability assumed for damages resulting from the use of the information contained herein.

ISBN-13: 978-0-672-32940-1
ISBN-10: 0-672-32940-9

Library of Congress Cataloging-in-Publication Data

MacIntyre, Peter.

Zend Studio for eclipse developer's guide / Peter MacIntyre, Ian Morse.

p. cm.

Includes index.

ISBN-13: 978-0-672-32940-1 (pbk.)

1. Zend Studio. 2. PHP (Computer program language) 3. Web site development. 4. Debugging in computer science. I. Morse, Ian. II. Title.

QA76.73.P224M34 2008

006.7'6–dc22

2008004996

Printed in the United States of America

First Printing March 2008

Trademarks

All terms mentioned in this book that are known to be trademarks or service marks have been appropriately capitalized. Pearson cannot attest to the accuracy of this information. Use of a term in this book should not be regarded as affecting the validity of any trademark or service mark.

Warning and Disclaimer

Every effort has been made to make this book as complete and as accurate as possible, but no warranty or fitness is implied. The information provided is on an "as is" basis. The authors and the publisher shall have neither liability nor responsibility to any person or entity with respect to any loss or damages arising from the information contained in this book or programs accompanying it.

Bulk Sales

Pearson offers excellent discounts on this book when ordered in quantity for bulk purchases or special sales. For more information, please contact

U.S. Corporate and Government Sales
1-800-382-3419
corpsales@pearsontechgroup.com

For sales outside the U.S., please contact

International Sales
international@pearson.com

Associate Publisher
Mark Taub

Development Editor
Michael Thurston

Managing Editor
Patrick Kanouse

Project Editor
Mandie Frank

Copy Editor
Charles Hutchinson

Indexer
Ken Johnson

Proofreader
Susan Eldridge

Technical Editor
Bryon Poehlman

Publishing Coordinator
Vanessa Evans

Designer
Gary Adair

Safari
BOOKS ONLINE
ENABLED

The Safari® Enabled icon on the cover of your favorite technology book means the book is available through Safari Bookshelf. When you buy this book, you get free access to the online edition for 45 days. Safari Bookshelf is an electronic reference library that lets you easily search thousands of technical books, find code samples, download chapters, and access technical information whenever and wherever you need it.

To gain 45-day Safari Enabled access to this book:

- Go to http://www.informit.com/onlineedition
- Complete the brief registration form
- Enter the coupon code **SQKH-6LAJ-WU28-6CJI-MZHC**

If you have difficulty registering on Safari Bookshelf or accessing the online edition, please email customer-service@safaribooksonline.com.

❖

This book is dedicated to my son, Simon Peter MacIntyre, who is about to enter the "real world" as a Millennium Kid. He has demonstrated a keen interest in web development and specifically PHP. Simon, I hope that this book will further your interest in this great unbounded world of information technology. I know your ideas, aspirations, and accomplishments will far exceed my own. I love you, son!

—Peter B. MacIntyre

I would like to thank my wife, Susan, for her support, encouragement, and patience as this book was being written. My portions of this book are dedicated to her.

—Ian D. Morse

❖

Contents at a Glance

Table of Contents

Foreword

As an extensible tool integration platform, Eclipse has spawned the creation of a large and vibrant open source and commercial software ecosystem. Zend Studio for Eclipse is a significant addition to that ecosystem.

From the perspective of our community, the PDT (PHP Development Tools) project is an important new addition to Eclipse. Although we are best known for our Java IDE, the Eclipse community has long since evolved into something much more interesting. I believe that it is fair to say that today Eclipse has become the leading open source tooling integration platform. Our goals are not to simply create an integrated development environment (IDE), but to create a platform for many IDEs. Even more challenging, our community is creating a tooling platform that supports the creation of all types of software tools, extending well beyond the scope of traditional developer tools. Today at Eclipse, you can find tools that span the complete software development lifecycle from modeling and design to data analysis to development to testing and monitoring.

But amongst many developers, the perception remains that Eclipse is a "Java thing". While it is true that most of the code built at Eclipse is written in Java, our goals have always been to provide development tools that span as many programming languages and platforms as possible. For example, our C/C++ Development Tools (CDT) project has achieved a lot of success in the Linux and embedded development worlds. The PDT project upon which Zend Studio for Eclipse is based is a further (and critical) evolution of this vision.

As one of the largest and fastest growing web development languages, PHP has quickly grown to a mainstream enterprise development language and platform. In addition to being the web development language of choice for many sites (we use it ourselves at www.eclipse.org!), it is also the technology that underlies many of the Web's most important wiki and content management systems. As an everyday example, consider the very popular Wikipedia site which is built on MediaWiki which is, in turn, based on PHP. Another very popular PHP-based web property is Facebook. There are too many examples to possibly list here, but the point is that PHP as a language and as a platform is firmly woven into the fabric of our everyday use of the Web. And it has achieved that in just slightly over 10 years of existence (starting from PHP 3). At the time of writing, PHP is currently the fourth most popular programming language on the planet (source: http://www.tiobe.com/tpci.htm). In fact, the now-classic combination of PHP with Linux, Apache and MySQL (commonly referred to as the LAMP stack) is widely credited with the rapid growth of dynamic web properties over the past decade. It is a proven stack which meets the business and technical needs of many of the most important websites that we all use on a day-to-day basis.

The Eclipse community itself may be used as a proof point of PHP's adoption and success. While the Eclipse platform and projects are implemented in Java, if you take a look at the many web properties run by the Eclipse Foundation, they are all implemented in PHP.

PDT provides you, the PHP developer, with the tools you need to build, debug and deploy PHP applications.

But just as importantly, because PDT is based on the Eclipse platform, it provides you with not only great PHP development tools but with a tools platform that you can use to integrate with other Eclipse-based products and open source plug-ins. PDT is designed to be an open extensible system, and a large measure of its future success will be growth in the number of its own ecosystem of Eclipse plug-ins, both open source and commercial. But in addition, there are a great many existing Eclipse plug-ins that you can draw upon to extend your tooling environment. To tap into this world of Eclipse extensions, take a look at our Eclipse Plug-In Central website (also implemented on PHP) which can be found at:

http://www.eclipseplugincentral.com/

Hopefully both the *Zend Studio for Eclipse Developers Guide* and the PDT toolset will make you a more productive PHP developer. But please remember that Eclipse is all about active community involvement, and we hope to welcome you soon as an active contributor to PDT and other projects at Eclipse. As you work with PDT and the capabilities described in this book, I'd encourage you to communicate your successes back to the community, and perhaps consider contributing any interesting extensions you may develop. The PDT website may be found here:

http://www.eclipse.org/pdt/

It includes pointers to the PDT newsgroup—where you can communicate and share your results with other PDT users and adopters—and pointers to the Eclipse installation of Bugzilla, where you can contribute your bugs, comments and patches.

Mike Milinkovich
Executive Director,
Eclipse Foundation

About the Authors

Peter MacIntyre has over 19 years of experience in the information technology industry, primarily in the area of software development. He is a Zend Certified Engineer, and his technical skill set includes several web development languages, client/server tools, and relational database systems such as PHP, PowerBuilder, Visual Basic, Active Server Pages, and CA-Visual Objects.

MacIntyre has contributed to several books, including *Using Visual Objects*, *Using PowerBuilder 5*, *ASP.NET Bible*, *The Web Warrior Guide to Web Programming*, and *Programming PHP 5*, 2nd edition, and is a former contributing editor to the online and in-print magazine called *php | architect*. He has spoken several times at North American and international computer conferences, including CA-World in New Orleans, USA; CA-TechniCon in Cologne, Germany; and CA-Expo in Melbourne, Australia.

MacIntyre lives and works in Prince Edward Island, Canada, where he runs his own part-time software company called Paladin Business Solutions (www.paladin-bs.com)

Ian Morse has a bachelor's degree in computer science from the University of Prince Edward Island. He has experience working in both the public and private sectors. For the past several years, he has worked as a private consultant and web system developer under the name of geckoWARE.

Acknowledgments

First, I would like to acknowledge my family for supporting my authoring efforts. My wife, Dawn, who is always there for me to talk to about life and the struggles we face together, I love you! To my kids who are almost all grown up and on their own now, thanks for the gray hairs and the experiences that we have all shared together.

Further from home, I would like to thank Mr. Michel Gerin, a former employee of Zend Corporation who first considered me as an author for this book. Much appreciated, Michel!

Also, naturally, thanks to my coauthor Ian, whom I have known for several years even though we are still both fairly young. Ian has been a great new author; he was always keen to do the work and put in the effort to get this project out the door. Ian, I also wish you every success as a new father.

Next on the list is Yossi Leon, the project development lead on this NEON effort. Yossi has spent countless hours answering our questions and listening to our feedback on the product and how the book needs to relate very closely with it. We met in New York City in December 2006 to discuss the early plans for this book, and even though you gave us poor subway station directions, we made it back home. Thanks, Yossi, I now consider you to be one of my closer friends in the technology industry.

Mark de Visser, Chief Marketing Officer at Zend, has supported us in this effort from the beginning. At times difficult to get in contact with, Mark has offered some great marketing ideas for this book, and I certainly appreciate your contributions and support.

I also promised Rock Mutchler that I would be sure to give him a nod for his early assistance in this book. He was originally going to be a coauthor with us but, because of other commitments, was not able to stay with this project. Thanks for your early assistance, Rock.

Bryon Poehlman, our technical editor, is a long-time friend of mine, and I am certainly glad that he was able to help us out on this project. The trips to New Orleans for technology conferences with you, Bryon, will always be a treasured memory of mine. Thanks for your contributions to this book and to my life!

Lastly, and certainly not least, the folks at Pearson Education have to be given a big thank you. Specifically, Mark Taber and Vanessa Evans, thanks for your interest in this title from the beginning and your patience with us as we tried to write a book based on a moving target. All the editors and graphics people at Pearson also deserve a thank you; this book would not have been possible without your skills and efforts.

—Peter MacIntyre

This book is the result of months (years for some) of hard work by countless people. I would like to thank my coauthor, Peter MacIntyre, for asking for my help with the writing and for taking care of most of the administrative work. Of course, this book could not have been written without the support of Zend. Yossi Leon tirelessly answered our questions and helped immeasurably with fine-tuning the table of contents.

Many thanks go to our publisher, Pearson Education. Vanessa Evans and Mark Taber kept our ship on its course. It has been a pleasure working with you.

—Ian Morse

We Want to Hear from You!

As the reader of this book, *you* are our most important critic and commentator. We value your opinion and want to know what we're doing right, what we could do better, what areas you'd like to see us publish in, and any other words of wisdom you're willing to pass our way.

You can email or write us directly to let us know what you did or didn't like about this book—as well as what we can do to make our books stronger.

Please note that we cannot help you with technical problems related to the topic of this book, and that we might not be able to reply to every message.

When you write, please be sure to include this book's title and authors as well as your name and phone or email address.

Email: feedback@pearsontechgroup.com
Mail: Pearson Technology Group
800 East 96th Street
Indianapolis, IN 46240 USA

Reader Services

For more information about this book, see http://www.informit.com/store/product.aspx?isbn=0672329409 where you can find the source code used as well as any errata. The website also includes links to a more complete website that is maintained by the authors.

Introduction

PHP is currently the most widely used programming language on the Web with over 5 million developers, responsible for 40% of existing web applications. The simplicity of PHP has led to more than 20 million domains written in PHP, with growth continuing. When compared with other languages for achieving the development of a web application, PHP has proven to have tremendous advantage with its simplicity, in terms of the amount of work required and the potential complexity of its code.

The need for an editor or a development environment to create web applications with a short "time to market" is obvious, and different possibilities are available today for the PHP developer community. The possibilities can be categorized into three main groups in which each group introduces a different set of features, addresses different needs, and subsequently is tagged with a different pricing.

The first group, generally known as *Simple Editors*, includes the most basic feature set, such as syntax highlighting as part of the editor. Some of these editors come with the different operating systems, and some are the evolution of those (for example, NotePad and NotePad++). This group of editors usually doesn't include management tools like debugging or code analyzing tools, and is good for quick pinpoint development rather than large and complex web applications. Most of these editors are free of charge.

Basic Integrated Development Environments (IDEs) are the second group; they include an additional layer of features. These features can include basic debugging, project management, and several analysis tools. Some of these editors are free of charge, and sometimes they are even open source products.

The last group, known as *Professional IDEs*, includes all-in-one solution products. These development environments generally include development, management, analyzing, debugging, and deployment tools. The complete feature set in these products provides the capability to support full product development life cycles, starting from the development of the code until the deployment to the production server. A Professional IDE is a commercial product and can include an installation wizard and product support as well.

Over the years we can see a marked increase in the number of developers moving to professional IDEs from the basic editors. The need for team support, deployment tools, and quick development has convinced many companies to invest their money in the purchase of development tools with a quick return of both investment and productivity.

The gap between simple and professional IDEs can also enable some companies to provide a product free as a simple, initial solution. There may also be the option to pay for upgrades and thus be entitled to then use a professional IDE, but this is not always the case.

Zend Studio for Eclipse is based on the Eclipse technology in general and the PHP Development Tools (PDT) project in particular. The decision to develop based on the Eclipse technology was made because there are a few million developers who use Eclipse or Eclipse-based products. Many of those developers are looking at PHP as a way of developing rich Internet applications, and they simply wanted PHP support in Eclipse.

Zend has been working on Zend Studio for Eclipse for quite some time parallel to the development of the PDT Eclipse project. The product has been released a few times to a close group of beta testers to ensure the product stability and user interface usability and to gather feedback and bugs.

This book's authors, Peter MacIntyre and Ian Morse, who have vast experience in the PHP world and have been developing with Zend Studio for Eclipse in the past year, provide a great understanding of Zend Studio for Eclipse and its functionality.

The book provides explanations and instructions on how to use the best professional PHP IDE available today! In this book you also learn to develop web applications in the easiest and most productive way because this book not only introduces you to the many wonders of Zend Studio for Eclipse, but also guides you in developing a small web Customer Relationship Management (CRM) application.

Yossi Leon
Product Manager, Development Tools
Zend Technologies, Inc., the PHP Company

A First Look at Zend Studio for Eclipse

You have made a very important decision: You have selected to use Zend Studio for Eclipse as your PHP (Hypertext Preprocessor - a recursive acronym) development environment. This is a big step forward to you if you are not familiar with the workings of the Eclipse environment. Also, if you're familiar with Eclipse, many enhancements to the basic environment can be brought to bear on the development effort.

This chapter introduces you to the overall workings of Zend Studio for Eclipse and gives you the basic foundation so that you become familiar with the terms used and the concepts that are common throughout. By the end of this chapter, you should know what a perspective is, what a view is, and what a project is. We first look at the basic terms used within Zend Studio for Eclipse; these terms are intermixed with some screenshots of what you should be seeing. After that portion of the chapter, we take you on a quick tour of the overall environment within Zend Studio for Eclipse (preferences) so that you will be able to be somewhat fruitful with this product by the end of the chapter.

View

A *view* is any subwindow that gives you information on a certain application development topic. For example, the PHP Explorer view is the view into the project management portion of the Zend Studio for Eclipse environment. Many different views are available within Zend Studio for Eclipse, and following is a partial list with a brief description of what each view is designed for so that you have an idea of what a view is all about:

- **PHP Explorer View** ★ —This is the main project management view in Zend Studio for Eclipse. Here, you open new projects, import existing projects, create new files for a project, and so on.

- **Outline View** — This view outlines the objects, methods (class functions), properties, and user-defined functions and constants in the file that currently has focus. You can click on a certain item in this view and be taken directly to the code that is defined within the selected item (if the Link with Editor option is turned on).

- **PHP Project Outline View** — This view has the same functionality as the Outline view except that its scope is projectwide.
- **PHP Function View** — This view shows all the native functions within PHP in alphabetical order and allows you to import their syntax directly into your code by double-clicking on the function of your choice. It also allows you to look up any documentation on a selected function in PHP's online manual by right-clicking on a function.
- **Problems View** ★ — Zend Studio for Eclipse constantly scans open code files looking for problems to report to the developer. It uses this view to report any problems that are encountered.
- **Tasks View** ★ — In this view you can assign tasks that need to be accomplished. There are three levels of status codes, and you can be specific about what section of code needs attention.
- **Browser Output View** — This view shows the output of a PHP file that is run within Zend Studio for Eclipse.

Now that you're familiar with some of the views, let's look at a few screenshots to see what they look like. The items with the asterisks in the preceding list are the views shown in Figures 1.1 through 1.3.

Figure 1.1   PHP Explorer view looking at two projects.

Description ▲	Resource	Path	Location
⊟ Errors (6 items)			
⊗ strict-error : var: Deprecated. Please use	formatter.php	ExampleProject	line 9
⊗ strict-error : var: Deprecated. Please use	formatter.php	ExampleProject	line 10
⊗ strict-error : var: Deprecated. Please use	formatter.php	ExampleProject	line 11
⊗ strict-error : var: Deprecated. Please use	formatter.php	ExampleProject	line 12
⊗ strict-error : var: Deprecated. Please use	formatter.php	ExampleProject	line 13
⊗ strict-error : var: Deprecated. Please use	formatter.php	ExampleProject	line 14
⊞ Warnings (100 of 151 items)			

Figure 1.2   Problems view showing errors.

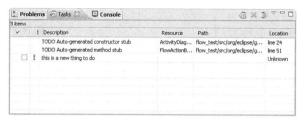

Figure 1.3   Tasks view showing three tasks,
one of which is marked as urgent.

Zend Studio for Eclipse has many different views, and it would be difficult to show and discuss them all at this early stage. However, we discuss every view during the course of this book. If you want to see a list of all the available views, as in Figure 1.4, select the Window menu and then select Show View, Other.

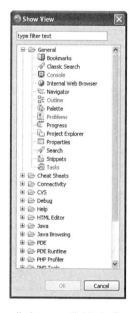

Figure 1.4   Listing all views available in Zend Studio for Eclipse.

Another aspect of views that you may find helpful at the outset of your relationship with Zend Studio for Eclipse is the concept of *fast views*. You can accomplish this by right-clicking on the view in question and then selecting Fast View from the pop-up menu. When you make this selection, the view that you're working on minimizes itself to the taskbar at the bottom of the Integrated Development Environment (IDE). This action effectively takes that view out of the picture, but you can reactivate it quickly (thus the name) by clicking on its icon in the taskbar. It then becomes a toggle view of sorts, and you can restore it to its original setting as a normal view by turning off the Fast View property; to do this, you right-click on its Fast View icon in the taskbar.

Perspectives

You may have heard the saying that goes "Everyone has a different perspective." This expression has great meaning and power within the Zend Studio for Eclipse environment. In the context of the Zend Studio for Eclipse product, a *perspective* is simply a collection of similar views that can be used to accomplish a specific task. In the typical opening of Zend Studio for Eclipse, you are presented with the default PHP perspective, which has nine different views distributed on the IDE screen. The PHP perspective (or collection of views) is predefined for you by Zend and is organized to help you develop PHP applications, write code, and manage development projects. Figure 1.5 shows you this perspective.

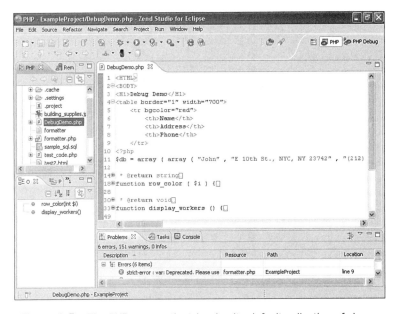

Figure 1.5   The PHP perspective showing its default collection of views.

Many predefined perspectives are available to you within Zend Studio for Eclipse. There is a debugging perspective, Database Development Perspective, What You See Is What You Get (WYSIWYG) HTML perspective, and PHP Profile perspective, just to name a few. To see the whole list of perspectives predefined for you, select Window, Open Perspective, Other.

Another great thing about these perspectives is that you can adjust them to suit your own development styles. So if you want the Task and Problems views above the Code Writing view, you are free not only to move these views around, but also to save these adjusted perspectives and use them from that point on as your new default perspective. All you have to do is move the views around your Zend Studio for Eclipse IDE and when you have them where you want them, select Window, Save Perspective As and name your new perspective. Figure 1.6 shows the adjusted PHP perspective just described with the Problems and Tasks views moved to the top. Also notice that a toolbar, called the Perspectives toolbar, is available on the right side of the IDE; this is a collection of icons that allows you to quickly switch between recently used perspectives.

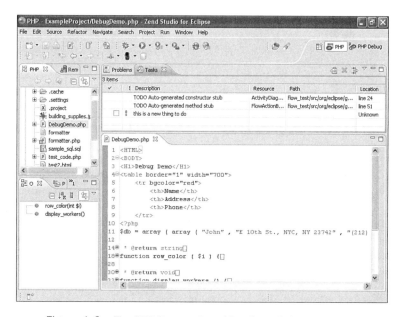

Figure 1.6   The PHP Perspective with adjusted view locations.

Perspectives are not only related to the collection of views that you have open, but are also able to manage (in a limited way) the menus and toolbar items that are associated with them. To see this level of customization control, select Window, Customize Perspective. A dialog similar to that shown in Figure 1.7 appears. Here, you can adjust certain menu items and toolbar icons that you may not want to appear within your personal perspective, or you may want to add some of these items to it.

Note

It is suggested that you save a standard perspective, like the default PHP perspective, with a new name and then add or remove menu items and icons to see how Zend Studio for Eclipse reacts. Then, when you have a solid layout that you are happy with, you can save it one last time.

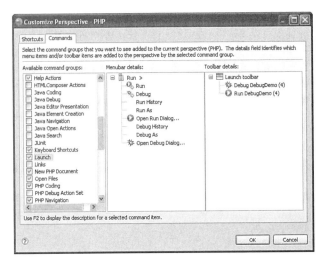

Figure 1.7   The Customize Perspective dialog.

Outline View

The next major portion of Zend Studio for Eclipse that you should be aware of is the Outline view. This view is like no other, and it will be of great import to you after you learn the ins and outs of it. The Outline view attempts to display a tree view of any entities that it can find within the file that currently has focus. So if a JavaScript file is open in the code editor and is in focus, the Outline view categorizes any functions or variable definitions that are found and organizes them in the aforementioned tree view. If the file is an object-oriented PHP code file, the outline view redefines itself to list any class definitions, methods (class functions), properties (class variables), functions, and defined constants. When these items are categorized and listed, if the Link with Editor option is turned on, clicking on any of these items brings them into focus within the code editor. Figure 1.8 shows the Outline view in action with a PHP class definition file open.

The Outline view is one of the views that you will use most often during your code development, so it would be in your best interest to become familiar with it as soon as possible. Imagine having a large object-oriented PHP project with lots of classes, methods, and properties and then having to locate a certain method to adjust its workings. The Outline view not only organizes the information for you, but also takes you to the code file and exact line of code in question after you locate it in that view.

An interesting addition to this Outline view is that when you are looking at a "raw" HTML file, the view also lists every tag that it can and organizes them into a tree view, as in Figure 1.9.

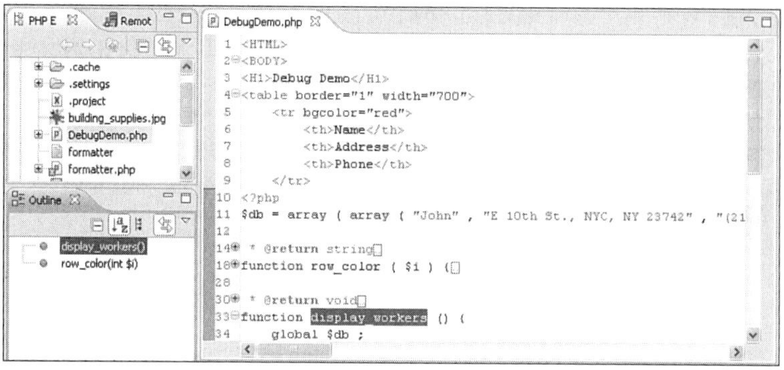

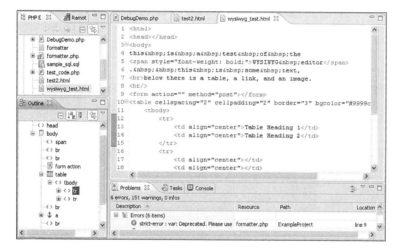

Figure 1.8   Outline view with PHP class method (function) highlighted.

Figure 1.9   Outline view with "raw" HTML file open.

Working Sets

The next concept or general-use approach to Zend Studio for Eclipse that you would be well served to become familiar with is that of working sets. A *working set* is merely a collection of files or open projects that you can arrange together and give a specific name. You can think of this collection as a perspective for projects or files. If you have a few files from two or more related projects that you want to work on, you can create a working set of them and then do what is required to those files without the clutter of having open all the files from all the projects.

To define a working set, select Window, Working Sets, Edit. If there are already defined working sets, you can select them here, or you can click on the New button and begin to define your own working set. Clicking on the New button starts a small wizard process. First, you select the type of working set that you want (for now, just select a PHP working set); next, you can select projects or individual files for inclusion into your working set that you will also have to name. Figure 1.10 shows a working set being defined and named.

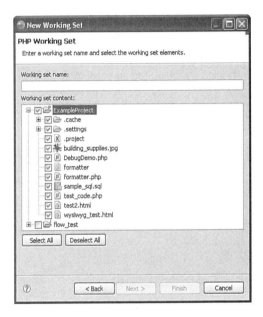

Figure 1.10   Defining a new working set.

You may find that over time it will make your work easier to define working sets when you're working on large-sized projects. These working sets will help you to focus on the sections of the project that you want to deal with instead of taking up Zend Studio for Eclipse resources and desktop space loading in a large number of files for a project when you want to work only on a subset of a project.

Code Editor

The most important part of Zend Studio for Eclipse is, quite possibly, the code editor. This is the main view in which you do all your code writing, editing, and debugging. It won't take you long to become accustomed to seeing this editor because it is front and center in every perspective. This view is the actual hub of Zend Studio for Eclipse. Figure 1.11 shows a typical PHP file open and editable within the code editor.

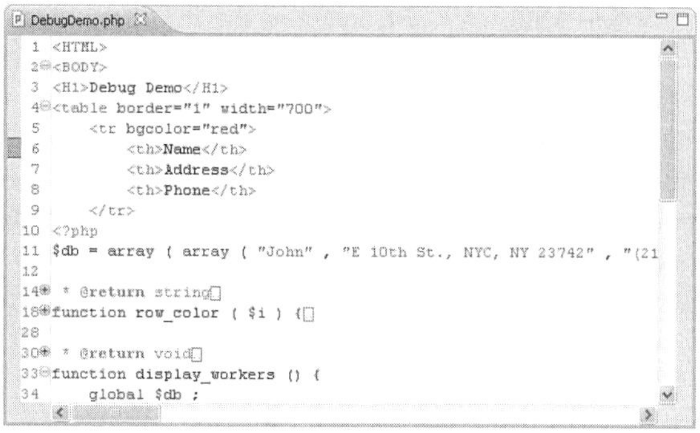

Figure 1.11   The code editor with some PHP code being edited.

Depending on the type of file being edited, the code editor adjusts itself to try to make as many editing options available to you. For instance, if you're editing an HTML file, you are given a different toolbar than you see if you are just coding a PHP file. The HTML appearance gives you access to a WYSIWYG feature where you can design table layout and so forth. Because this is not within the context of a PHP file, the editor does not show this to you in that situation.

The code editor also has many subtle features; code completion is one of them. When you're writing code, the *code completion* feature allows you to complete a command or tag by offering anything that is close in proximity to help speed up the writing process. Figure 1.12 shows the code completion offering made in the PHP context when only num was entered into the code editor. If you see this code assistant when there are many possible hits for it, a full pop-up list of all possibilities is displayed to you and is narrowed down to the more accurate selection as you continue to type your code.

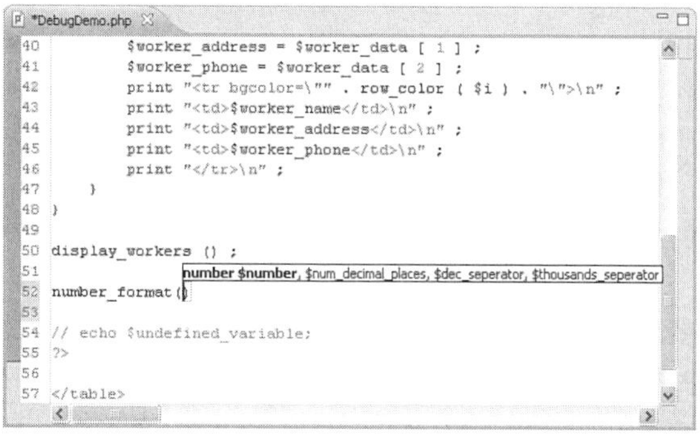

Figure 1.12   The code completion assistant showing the code context for the `number_format` PHP function.

The code editor also offers a number of features in the thin strip that runs top to bottom on its left side. Here, notice line numbers (unless the feature is turned off) and little icons that represent code errors, warnings, or even breakpoints (used in debugging). If you right-click while hovering over this vertical strip, a pop-up menu appears, showing you most of the options available to you. Also, in that same vicinity are little plus and minus icons that signify the capability of the code editor to "fold" code. Folding, in effect, reduces the code in view by collapsing it based on class and function definitions, similar in concept to collapsing and expanding a tree-view interface. You see the code that you want and are not bothered by code that you know is working fine yet may be taking up needed screen real estate.

Note

This code folding is also available to certain HTML elements like the head, body, and table tags.

Figure 1.13 shows a sample of some of these icons with an error(red *x*'s), plus a few break points (blue circles).

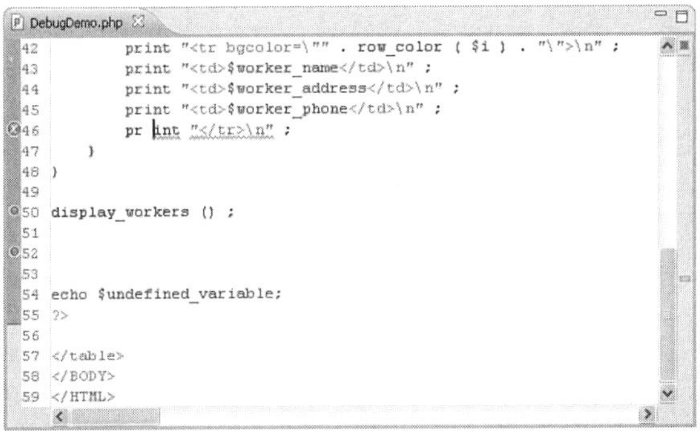

Figure 1.13   The code editor showing an error and breakpoint icons.

A lot more can be done with the code editor, and these tasks are covered in more depth throughout the book, more specifically in Chapter 4, "The Code Editor."

Preferences

Zend Studio for Eclipse has many different settings and options available within its overall environment. This means that you, as the software developer, also have many options available to you in the way you make Zend Studio for Eclipse perform. There are IDE appearance options, code editing options, file and project options, debugging options, and server definition options, just to name a few. To see these options listed in a tree-view layout and to be able to manipulate their values, you simply need to open the Preferences window, shown in Figure 1.14, by selecting Window, Preferences.

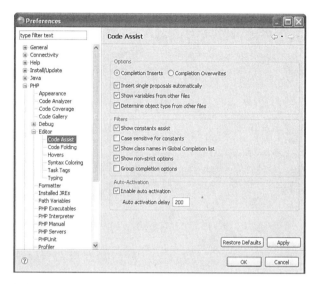

Figure 1.14   Zend Studio for Eclipse's Preferences management window.

> **Note**
>
> Don't worry about the details of the preferences for now because Chapter 3, "Environmental Settings," is dedicated to managing preferences.

After you open the Preferences window, you can see all the options broken down for you by category in the tree-view format, as mentioned. There is also a Filter option available at the top of the window; if you know the general topic of the setting that you want to manipulate, you can filter for it here.

Summary

This chapter provided a brief overview of the major sections and concepts available to you in the Zend Studio for Eclipse environment. This information should get you operational or at least familiar with the Zend Studio for Eclipse environment so that you can begin using the IDE and become somewhat productive with it. We recommend that you read the next three chapters to get a much better handle on the code editor, project settings, and environmental settings so that your productivity can soar!

2

Creating Projects

As with just about any Integrated Development Environment (IDE) on the market today, users are guided into the concept of doing their work in blocks or groups of tasks, also known as *projects*. Projects are also naturally the central control point to creating a web application in Zend Studio for Eclipse, so this chapter guides you through creating and managing projects.

Projects Wizard

Zend Studio for Eclipse has added a project creation wizard to its environment to help you get underway with new projects. When you decide to start a new project, you can use this wizard to guide you through the different options available within Zend Studio for Eclipse. Before you start a new Zend Studio for Eclipse project, you should take some time to consider its features in terms of the following:

- Where will the project files be stored?
- Will a team of developers work on this project?
- Will the location of the project files be important to testing while in development?
- What supporting libraries will be needed for the new project?

There are other unique questions that you will want to have answered for each particular project, but the preceding questions, when answered, give you a good starting point to almost any Zend Studio for Eclipse project.

To start a new Zend Studio for Eclipse project, right-click on the PHP Explorer view in the top-left section of the IDE and select New, or open the File menu and select New. Within this menu, you have the option to launch a few different wizards, but for now just select the PHP Project option. This selection is shown in Figure 2.1.

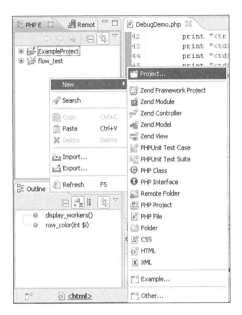

Figure 2.1   Launching the PHP Project Wizard.

After you select the PHP Project option from the menu, the corresponding wizard is launched. In this option window, some of those initial questions are now answered. The first thing the wizard needs is the name of the new project in question. For this example, we will name the project "PHP Sample", so this name will appear in the PHP Explorer when the wizard is finished.

The next option that you are presented with is choosing where you will be storing the contents of this project. In other words, where will you be saving your project files? In this matter, there are some factors to consider. If you take the directory path offered to you by the wizard (and you have not changed any of the Workspace settings), your project files will be stored in a rather obscure location. The file path offered to me was `C:Documents and SettingspetermacZendWorkspacesDefaultWorkspace PHP_Sample`.

It would be better for the project to have its own location under a less complex file path for two reasons: Finding the path is easier if it is not buried so deeply in the file system, and if you want to run any of the files within the browser and you have a local or networked access to a web server, it would be beneficial to save all your files within the file structure of a web server. This also allows you to skip the step of "publishing" the files each time you want to review them in a browser. Therefore, I chose to save my project files in my local copy of Apache at `C:Program FilesApache GroupApachehtdocsPHP_Sample`. And although this path is rather lengthy, it will be available to my localhost browser for testing as I build the web application.

These options are not the only ones offered to you in the initial step of the PHP Project Wizard. The next block of information offered to you, titled PHP Version, is the ability to override the Workspace settings for this particular project. The settings in the Workspace are generally systemwide options that are expected to apply to all projects within the Zend Studio for Eclipse IDE. Here, though, you are given the option to override those options because the project that you are now defining may have some special requirements. Figure 2.2 shows these options with the settings I chose.

Figure 2.2   Changing the default settings on the PHP Project Wizard.

If you indeed decide to override the Workspace settings, you need to initially mark the Enable Project Specific Settings checkbox. When you do this, the options under the control of this checkbox are activated and await your alterations. In this case, only two options are available: to tell Zend Studio for Eclipse that you want to use a different version of PHP and whether you want your project to be able to use ASP tags as PHP tags. For our example, keep the Workspace default project settings as they are already defined.

When you have finished with all the options on this window of the wizard, you can click on the Next button at the bottom to continue the wizard's progress. Or, if you have no other needs in defining this particular project, you can click Finish.

If you clicked on the Next button, the next screen in the Project Creation Wizard is displayed. On this screen you can identify any supporting libraries or projects that you want to use in conjunction with this new project. For example, in this project we identified the *fpdf library* (a free PHP library used to build dynamic PDF files for websites) as being required, as shown in Figure 2.3.

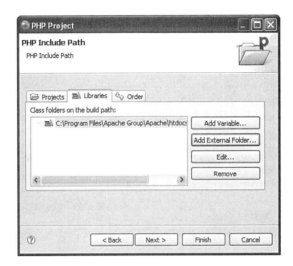

Figure 2.3   Identifying required supporting libraries for a new project.

After all the parts of the project are identified, click on the Finish button, and the project is created. There are only these two main windows in the Project Creation Wizard, but a lot is accomplished. The newly created project is now shown in the PHP Explorer. You can create your PHP files and edit them within this new project context.

Zend Framework Project

You may want to create a different kind of PHP project within Zend Studio for Eclipse that makes proper use of the Zend Framework library. In this instance all you have to do is select File, New, Zend Framework Project in the menu system. The resulting wizard is almost identical in that you have to provide a project name and a project storage location. You also have the option to override the Workspace default project settings if you desire.

The difference then comes in the second screen of the wizard. On this screen, you are shown that the wizard has already included the Zend Framework Library for you. You can also add your own libraries if you want to at this stage. When you complete the wizard, Zend Studio for Eclipse does a little extra work for you in setting up a Model-View-Controller (MVC) environment for your newly created project in the context of the Zend Framework. As you can see in Figure 2.4, the project is created with the library attached and the MVC framework in place.

> **Note**
>
> For more coverage about the Zend Framework Library and MVC concepts, see Chapter 17, "Designing the Project."

Figure 2.4   A Zend Framework Project skeleton has been created.

Multiproject Support

As you can see from Figure 2.4, another great feature is added to the Zend Studio for Eclipse environment: that of multiple concurrent project management. You can open and close as many projects as your development hardware and operating system allow. This capability is beneficial in that you can have code in one project that you want to have access to while you are working on a different project altogether. This feature alone is worth its weight in gold if you're a multitalented modern PHP developer, especially if you are also in a maintenance role supporting many web applications at the same time.

These projects can be expanded and collapsed at will and can even be temporarily removed from the PHP Explorer View if they are in the way. To remove a project from this viewer, simply select the project and right-click to bring up the pop-up menu. Then select Delete from that menu to remove the project from view. Be sure to select the correct option from the Confirm Project Delete dialog if you don't want to totally remove the project from the system.

To bring any existing project back into the PHP Explorer View, right-click on any whitespace in the viewer and select Import from the pop-up menu. In the Import dialog that is displayed, select Existing Projects into Workspace under the General folder. This brings up a browse dialog where you can list all your existing projects. Select the project that you want and click Finish. This brings the project back into the PHP Explorer view. Figure 2.5 shows the Open Project dialog with the existing projects that Zend Studio for Eclipse knows about. You can select multiple projects by clicking on their checkboxes.

All this opening and closing of existing projects can also be controlled through the drop-down menu (the PHP Explorer menu) that is at the immediate right of the PHP Explorer view and is identifiable by the white triangle pointing downward. When this menu is activated, you see a whole filtering capability that is also available. If you want to hide or show projects of different types, click the Filters menu item (second to last on the list) to open the project filtering window. As shown in Figure 2.6, this dialog allows you to filter on much more than just project files, and this capability further enhances your project management within Zend Studio for Eclipse.

Figure 2.5   Adding existing projects to the PHP Viewer.

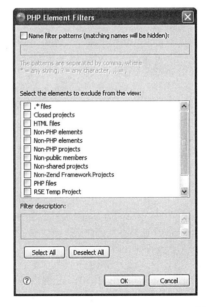

Figure 2.6   Assigning filter selections for the PHP Viewer.

Setting Up Working Sets

Working sets are another variation of the filtering process within Zend Studio for Eclipse. With working sets, you can have multiple projects open or even just one project open and simply request the IDE to show you only certain files from the project or projects that you currently have open. The benefit is that you may, for example, have two projects open and want to see only a single file from one of those projects instead of having the display "cluttered" with all the files of that project.

To set up a working set, pull down the view's menu and choose Select Working Set. In the dialog that appears, you can name and define your working set. If this is your first time using this dialog, nothing is shown in the list of existing working sets. Clicking on the New button starts a new working set wizard of sorts that allows you to define the type of working set that you want, whether it's PHP, Java, or others. In this case, select the PHP list item and click Next. The following dialog shows you all the PHP projects that you are currently working with in your overall environment and allows you to pick and choose what elements of each project you want to see in this newly defined working set. As shown in Figure 2.7, only a few files are selected from the ExampleProject, the entire project is selected for the Framework_Sample project, and the working set is named MyWorkingSet.

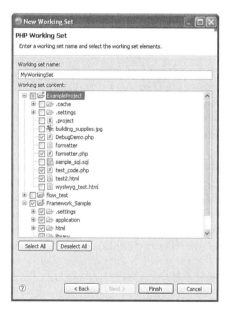

Figure 2.7   Defining a working set for the PHP Explorer.

When this working set is properly defined, named, and saved, you can select it by its name at any later time. So with this method of filtering, you are able to easily return to the project environment that you were working on at any time. Also, with multiple working sets, you can change to any of those predefined project environments at will.

> **Note**
>
> These working sets honor any filters that are currently active. If you are including files from a project that is closed and are filtering closed projects, those selected files within the working set are not shown.

Importing Projects

When you start working with Zend Studio for Eclipse, it is a rare case to start a brand-new project. Typically, you are working on existing projects or are at least doing maintenance on previously completed work. So there is obviously a need to be able to work on these existing projects within the Zend Studio for Eclipse environment.

Within the PHP Explorer view menu system is the capability to import existing projects. After right-clicking on the view's whitespace, you can select Import from the subsequent menu (this import process can also be started from the main File menu). Keep in mind, however, that you must have at least one project predefined within Zend Studio for Eclipse to be able to import into it. Again, after you select the Import option, you starting another wizard process. The initial dialog in the wizard offers many different kinds of import sources: archive files, breakpoints, other existing projects, and so on. The type of import process that we are describing here is that of a file system import. It is an existing PHP application that you now want to work on within the Zend Studio for Eclipse IDE. So, after selecting the File System option and clicking the Next button, you see a dialog like that shown in Figure 2.8.

When you see this dialog, you can navigate to the folder location for the files to be imported, select all the files (or a subset) in the selected folder, direct which folder these files should be imported into, and probably—and most importantly—direct the wizard to import only the files and folders selected, or take the entire folder structure of the incoming project. Additionally, you can filter the file types to be imported with the Filter Types button. Typically, you choose the Create Selected Folders Only option at the bottom of the dialog because the other option takes in the complete folder structure for the selected project.

After you have selected the files that you want and start the import process, Zend Studio for Eclipse brings those files into the designated project. These files are directly copied from the source folder, and no pointers are used to refer to the original files, so be sure that you do not continue to work on the files in the original folder at the same time because they will become immediately unsynchronized.

Figure 2.8   Importing an existing PHP
project into Zend Studio for Eclipse.

Exporting Projects

Exporting projects is just the opposite process to that discussed in the preceding section.
As before, a wizard process is activated when you select the Export menu option. Now
you can also select the files that you want or simply mark them all for export.
Designating the destination path and other options is similar to the import; one thing to
note here, though, is that if you select the top-level folder to be exported, that folder is
created under the named destination folder. So, to get around that, you have to select the
individual files at the top level and then any other folders subordinate to that.

The export wizard can employ many different formats and file types. Exporting
breakpoints in a project, for example, could be helpful for a team development project
that is being developed on two separate machines. The breakpoints can be exported and
then subsequently imported to the second machine, and both support developers can
watch the same code and make observations at the same time as the code runs and stops
at the same locations. The breakpoint file that is exported is actually a well-formed XML
file, as shown in Figure 2.9.

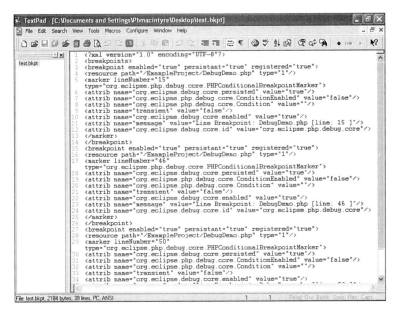

Figure 2.9   Exported breakpoints file in XML format.

Creating New Files

The main point behind the PHP Explorer is to maintain projects in a development environment. But what are projects without files? We have seen how these projects can import and export existing files, so in this section we cover the basic process of creating PHP files.

When adding a new PHP file to an existing project, right-click on the PHP Explorer's whitespace to bring up the Project menu. Once again, you can accomplish this task of creating a PHP file under the File menu; select New and then PHP File from the submenu. Yet another wizard interface is launched, and you are asked to supply the source folder (where the file will be stored after it is created) and the filename. Then you can click the Next button and select from the offering of file templates that are shown. Figure 2.10 shows this dialog.

> **Note**
>
> You can create and name your own file templates in the PHP section of the Preferences management area. See Chapter 3, "Environmental Settings," for more information on creating a file template.

Figure 2.10   Selecting a file template for a new PHP file.

Other file types can be created in this new file process, and depending on the file type that you specify, the Template dialog adjusts to those kinds of templates. So, for example, if you are creating a cascading style sheet (CSS) file, the Template dialog offers you any predefined CSS templates from which to choose.

After a file is created and assigned to a project, you can begin to write your code. Chapter 4, "The Code Editor," covers most of the tasks that you can accomplish within the code editor.

Using Link with Editor

Another feature that you may find handy within Zend Studio for Eclipse is its capability to switch the file in the editor (the viewer to the immediate right of the PHP Explorer on a typical perspective) on the fly. You see a menu option called Link with Editor, which is also identified by the menu icon of yellow arrows pointing left and right. When this toggle (on/off) feature is activated, if you change your highlighted file in the PHP Explorer (and the file is open in the code editor), that file is instantly brought into focus in the editor. This timesaving feature allows you to quickly jump between open files. This icon is also visible in the PHP Project Outline and Outline views that typically appear under the PHP Explorer view, so you can turn it on or off in either location and it will have the same effect.

Accessing Remote Files

Naturally, in today's broadband world of remote development, there are lots of examples of web development projects being created with team members in different cities all over the world. To that end, Zend Studio for Eclipse is able to work on remotely located files via either the FTP or SFTP protocols. In this chapter we discuss this topic briefly and define only an FTP connection. Chapter 13, "Version Control Integration," provides more in-depth coverage on remote development topics.

If you are going to make a connection to a remote location or server that is housing your project, you first have to tell Zend Studio for Eclipse where that server is located and any credentials that you need to gain access to it. If you are in the PHP perspective, you have to open the Remote Systems View, (if it is not already available behind the PHP Explorer View) by selecting Window, Show View, Remote Systems. The Show View dialog appears, as shown in Figure 2.11.

Figure 2.11   Selecting the Remote Systems
view from the Show View dialog.

After opening the Remote Systems View, you can define a remote site within it. Click on the first icon on its toolbar (green square with a yellow cross) or right-mouse on the view and select New, Connection to start the definition of an FTP server. When the New Site dialog appears, select the FTP Only option and click Next. The Remote FTP Only System Connection dialog appears, asking for your credentials, as is evident in Figure 2.12.

Once this connection is established (you will be asked for a username and password when you first make a connection), you can then browse the files on that remote server from within the Remote Systems View.

Figure 2.12 Providing the credentials for a remote FTP server connection.

Then to make this an even better option, Zend Studio for Eclipse allows you to create a remotely connected project. To do this, descend your file tree on the remote server to the location where a project would start (generally under the htdocs folder) then right-mouse on that folder and select Create Remote Project. This will then tell Zend Studio for Eclipse to create a project in the PHP Explorer View with the name of the server and the project folder combined into its name within that view (see Figure 2.13).

Note

You may also notice the console view appear and begin to become quite active during this process. This is merely the FTP connection information being displayed to you as you make connections and perform activities on the remote server.

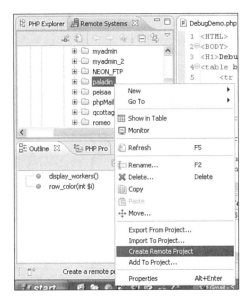

Figure 2.13   Creating a project in the PHP Explorer
View based on a remote FTP connection.

Summary

This chapter covered the basics of working with projects within the IDE environment and showed you some import and export methods. As well, multi-project editing and support was also discussed. Also, you briefly saw how to establish an FTP connection to a remote server and how to manage that connection within the context of local and remote projects. Once you get familiar with managing projects within Zend Studio for Eclipse, you will be well on your way to becoming extremely efficient in PHP development within this IDE.

3

Environmental Settings

This chapter discusses in detail all the options available to you in setting up the overall working environment of Zend Studio for Eclipse. The many options available cover subjects such as text color, tab styles, and server definitions.

First, however, there is a little more detailed coverage of the concepts of perspectives and how they can be employed to great gain in the context of the working environment of Zend Studio for Eclipse.

The Concept of Perspectives

As was discussed briefly in Chapter 1, "A First Look at Zend Studio for Eclipse," the concept of perspectives is helpful when you are using Zend Studio for Eclipse in different contexts and different stages of development. You should learn how easily you can define and utilize perspectives, and over time this ability should become second nature to you.

To begin with, you should look at the views that you want to have in focus. Then you can save those views and name them as your own perspective. To look at the views available, you can select Window, Show View, Other. A dialog appears, showing a list of all available views within Zend Studio for Eclipse. After you select the views that you want and arrange them on your screen, you can save that collection of views under a perspective name of your own choosing. To do this, select Window, Save Perspective As. Figure 3.1 shows the perspective naming dialog with the existing perspective names already listed.

The customization of the perspective does not end there. You can manage some of the toolbar icons and menu items that are connected to the perspective. To do this, select Window, Customize Perspective, or right-click on the perspective in question on its toolbar on the top-right side of the IDE and select Customize. Be sure that you name your new perspective uniquely before you change too many of its details just in case you are changing the options of a "stock" perspective that you don't want to change permanently. When the customization window opens, as shown in Figure 3.2, you can change any of the settings made available to you.

Figure 3.1   Saving a newly designed perspective.

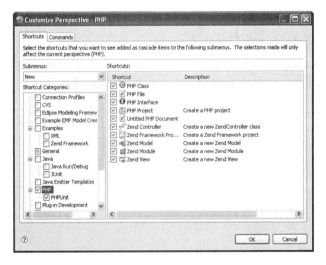

Figure 3.2   Customizing a newly created perspective.

On this customization window, you can control what menu items show up on each of three submenus: namely, the File, New menu; the Window, Open Perspective menu; and the Window, Show View menu. This is controlled through the Submenu drop-down list on the Shortcuts tab of the Customize Perspective window. When this drop-down is changed, the subcategories that are available adjust to the new context.

By switching to the Commands tab within this same customization window, you can then control both the menu item and toolbar item of other areas within Zend Studio for Eclipse (but only for the current perspective that you are customizing). Figure 3.3 shows the options for this tab. For example, if you turn on the HTML Composer Actions selection (as shown in the Figure 3.3), you activate the whole list of menu items under the Modify menu (which appears as a new top-level menu between the Project and Run menus), and you add a series of toolbar items that have their own toolbar at the top of the IDE (see Figure 3.4). Again, this happens only within the current perspective.

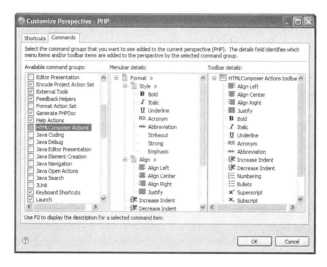

Figure 3.3   Customizing a newly created perspective.

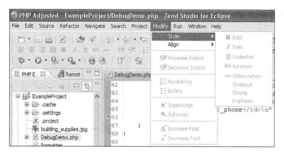

Figure 3.4   Newly added HTML Composer
Actions menu and toolbar items.

As you should be aware by now, the perspective feature of Zend Studio for Eclipse alone is extremely valuable to PHP developers. But, as you would expect from a modern computer programming interface, there is much more control at your fingertips. Enter Zend Studio for Eclipse Preferences.

Zend Studio for Eclipse Preferences

As with any major software product, you would expect to be able to have some sort of master control over its performance and look and behavior. Zend Studio for Eclipse is no exception; however, there are some differences between the Zend Studio for Eclipse product layer itself and the Eclipse foundation on which it is built. Under the Window menu, there is an item that opens up this Pandora's box of options: Preferences, located at the bottom of the menu displayed when you select Window. If you're not careful, you can get yourself into some trouble using this option. However, it's not too difficult to back yourself out of any corners that you may find yourself in.

Before we get too close to the details of the preferences, here are just a few words about the nature of the preferences. Some preferences have systemwide ramifications and some are quite specific to a certain topic or process. We guide you through most of these options in this chapter, but we merely mention some of these differences as such. Throughout the remainder of this chapter, we first discuss systemwide preferences and provide some detailed examples of them and then describe some specific preferences that affect how PHP is handled within Zend Studio for Eclipse itself. We deal with all other preference settings that may be adjusted depending on a certain topic inside that specific context.

Systemwide Preferences

In the following sections you will learn about much of the systemwide preferences that can be controlled in this IDE. Some are of a general nature that can affect the overall environment and some are more specific to a certain aspect of the IDE.

General

General preferences are exactly that—preferences to the overall environment of the Zend Studio for Eclipse IDE. With the highlight on the first item, named General, you can see the initial control area, as shown in Figure 3.5. Here, you are offered three checkbox controls and an Open Mode for item selections within the IDE. The three checkboxes are as follows:

- **Always Run in Background** — When this option is checked, the developer can continue working while longer running processes are executed in the background.
- **Keep Next/Previous Editor, View and Perspectives Dialog Open** — When this option is turned on, the Selection dialog for Editor, View, and Perspective Cycling stays open. When it is not selected, the dialog disappears. See the following note for a brief description on cycling.
- **Show Heap Status** — This option turns on an indicator that shows how much Java Heap memory is being used by Zend Studio for Eclipse. This indicator generally shows up in the bottom-right side of the display on the status bar. It also shows an icon that allows you to perform garbage collection.

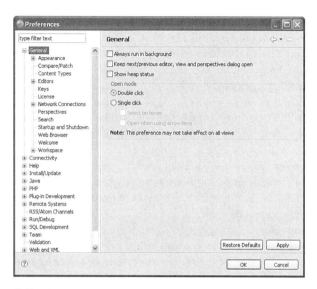

Figure 3.5   General Preferences window with fully expanded options list.

Note

Zend Studio for Eclipse gives you a relatively quick way to cycle through your open files in the editor with the Ctrl+F6 key combination. When you use this key sequence, a small dialog opens, showing all the currently open files (it stays open only when the Keep Next/Previous Part Dialog Open option is turned on in the General preferences). From this dialog, showing currently open views in Figure 3.6, you can then select one of these files to switch to. Selecting one of these files has the same result as clicking on the tab in the editor that was connected to an open file. The same functionality is available for Views (Ctrl+F7) and Perspectives (Ctrl+F8).

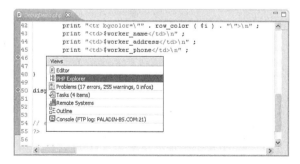

Figure 3.6   The View Cycling dialog.

Within the General Preferences window, the section labeled Open Mode in the lower half of the screen includes the options Double Click and Single Click. Choosing one of these options simply means that anywhere within the Zend Studio for Eclipse environment if you are selecting an item, you can either double-click or single-click on it. Also, within the Single Click option, you can control the hover action or the use of the arrow keys within that context.

If you click on the tree listing on the left side of this General Preferences window and select the Appearance item, you are given a host of options that, oddly enough, have an effect on the overall appearance of the Zend Studio for Eclipse IDE. The first option here simply allows you to select what I call a *master perspective*, or as Zend describes it, a *presentation*. If you change this to another option, Eclipse 2.1, and apply the changes, you see a totally different layout or presentation to the overall IDE. The perspective toolbar switches to a vertical orientation on the left side of the IDE, and other views are opened for you. If you don't like this presentation, change it back to the default in the preferences window. As another example, you can set the tabs that are on the top of the code editor to move to the bottom of the view if you prefer by selecting Bottom instead of Top in the Editor tab position. You can control the tab positions on the views as well as the editor if you want, and you can show or hide the descriptive text on the perspectives toolbar from this Appearance section.

Under the Appearance tree item are two subitems: Colors and Fonts and Label Decorations. Here, you can control the colors and font sizes of many of the editors, views, and wizards within Zend Studio for Eclipse. The Label Decorations simply add more information to a particular item. For example, if you turn on the PHP Problem Decorator and apply the changes, a small red *X* appears on any of the tree items in the PHP Explorer that may have problems. This is an aid in locating code issues within each tree item.

Note

Some of the General Preferences window tree items also have multiple tabs within them. For example, the General Appearance Compare/Patch Tree item has two tabs named General and Text Compare.

The next tree item under General Preferences is the Compare/Patch option. There are two tabs here to be concerned with. On the first tab, General, there are a number of checkboxes that you can adjust. Without going into each specific checkbox attribute, we can summarize all these options to have an effect on the comparison of versions of your code, whether with local histories of saved files or with CVS versions of your code. The second tab gives a little more visual clue as to what you will be adjusting. The Text Compare tab, shown in Figure 3.7, shows how a code comparison will look as you make some of the adjustments.

Figure 3.7   The Text Compare tab of the Preferences window.

On this tab, you can see that there are options in how the comparison between two files is displayed. If you want to see this in action, close your Preferences window and select a file in the code editor that you have been editing; right-click and then select Compare With, Local History from pop-up menu. If there is a local history, Zend Studio for Eclipse displays that with the comparison options that you have set.

The next option under the General Preferences is called Content Types; here, you simply assign different file types to various code styles. This is done via the file's extension. Most of these file associations are preset for you and don't really need to be adjusted, but the option is here for you just the same. For example, if you expand the text option and select the PHP tree item (PHP Content Type), you see a list of file associations that are preset (locked in) for Zend Studio for Eclipse. You have the option of adding new associations if you so choose.

Editors

The next major portion of the General Preferences window has to do with the editors that you will be using within Zend Studio for Eclipse. There is another section specific to PHP that directs the editor on a more specific level, but here, as the name implies, you can adjust the editors' features on a general level. Clicking on the Editors tree item itself reveals only a few options. You can turn on or off the tabs that appear on the top of each open file in the code editor by selecting the Show Multiple Editor Tabs option. Just above that, you can control the number of files that show up on the list of recently used files. The default is four, but I usually increase this number to at least eight when I'm working on a project of any significance.

The next items that you can control here are all related in some degree, and this is a feature that I am growing to like. You can tell Zend Studio for Eclipse to close open files automatically if more than a set number of files is currently open. If this option is turned on, the "first in, first out" rule is put into effect. If another file is opened in the editor, the oldest open file is closed (and you can control what happens to that file as it is being closed) and the newly requested file is opened. This method of file management can be well employed to maintain a "clean" development environment.

The next two tree items that are sublevels to the Editor level are File Associations and Structured Text Editors. In the File Associations area, you can control what happens when certain file types are encountered by Zend Studio for Eclipse. You can open specific editors, select *.sql from the File Types list, for example, and can have Zend Studio for Eclipse open the SQL Source Editor or the SQL Editor automatically. If you have two or more options per file type, it would be wise to select a default editor so that Zend Studio for Eclipse can open the files in the appropriate editor with little fuss.

After you have established some of your preferred file associations, you can look at the next option under the Editors branch called Structured Text Editors. This area of options relates to any editors that Zend Studio for Eclipse uses for structured text. This means any kind of code or HTML style of content that is not merely descriptive text but is more computer language based. In general terms, you can have matching brackets highlighted for you in these editors, you can have errors reported to you, you can be warned when unsupported content appears in those editors, and you can have code folding enabled where applicable. You can also control the color of the highlighted brackets if you want. The next tab within this same tree option is called Hovers; here, you can control how the hover pop-up help is displayed. For example, if you want to see problem help only when you hover over identified problem HTML code while holding down the Control (Ctrl) key, you can select the Problem Description item and add the pressed key modifier to it.

Still under the General Editors tree branch is a section called Text Editors. Without going into all the details here, you can control many features and options in relation to text editors within Zend Studio for Eclipse. For example, you can turn on or off the display of the line numbers, you can highlight the current line that the editor is focused on, and you can alter the width of the inserted spacing of the Tab key. Under the Annotations area, you can alter the colors and appearance of editor icons like the breakpoint, the error signifier (red underline squiggles), and code warnings, to name a few. You can even have your editors do spell checking, but this may not be advisable because a great deal of structured content like HTML and PHP uses short-formed and cryptic words for commands and functions. There would naturally be a lot of spelling errors in this context, so turn on this option with care and understanding of what it will do.

The next item under the General section of the Preferences is the keyboard mapping level. Under Keys, you can remap any keyboard key combination that is preset and make it your own. The neat thing here is that the keys are mapped in context. By that, I mean that you can map a key combination for one context of Zend Studio for Eclipse— Ctrl+B to build all code in a project, for example—and have the same key combination defined for another context—to turn on bold in the WYSIWYG editor. You can view these key mappings in the data grid and then alter them in the lower portion of this screen where the bindings are shown, see Figure 3.8.

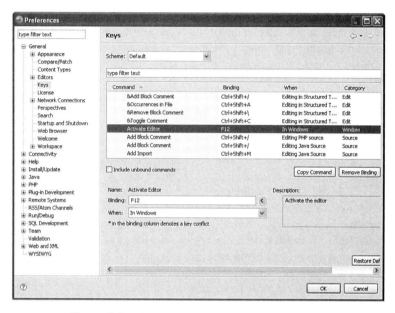

Figure 3.8   The Key mapping Preferences window.

The next branch on the General tree is the Perspectives branch. Here, you can control certain aspects of the preferences and how they react in the Zend Studio for Eclipse IDE. You can tell the perspective to open in a new window, open as a new view within an existing perspective, and you can tell Zend Studio for Eclipse to always open a certain perspective when a new project is started.

Below the Perspectives branch is the one called Search. Here, you can control how the Search feature works. You can tell it to reuse existing search windows on subsequent searches so that the desktop is less cluttered, you can colorize your results, and you can give the search view a default perspective in which to reside.

Following the Search branch is the Startup and Shutdown section. There is very little to control here except which Eclipse plug-ins should be active when Zend Studio for Eclipse starts and some workspace controls. One item that is recommended to be always active is the Confirm Exit When Closing Last Window option. This is a good safety feature to enable in Zend Studio for Eclipse because there is such potential to have a lot of views open at any one time, and you would not necessarily want to close down the whole environment when you want to close down only a few views.

The next branch, Web Browser, allows you to control the internal browser that Zend Studio for Eclipse uses. You can merely use the internal browser or select an external one to use. The three browser options that are initially offered to you are the default system browser (one your environment always launches when you ask for something from the Web), Firefox, and Internet Explorer. You can also define another browser to use if you like (Opera) and mark it as the default. Of course, the internal browser has a few advantages to that of the external one: You don't have to leave the Zend Studio for Eclipse environment, and it resolves and displays content more quickly.

The Welcome section is the place where you control how Zend Studio for Eclipse starts up and what features are displayed to you when you begin to use the IDE for your day's work. You can set it up to look almost browserlike with different quadrants for the initial splash screen, or you can simply ignore all this and get right into the IDE with the PHP perspective as your initial starting point.

The last area of interest under the General level of Preferences is labeled Workspace. On this branch you can set some overall workspace features such as when to build your projects (automatically) and whether you should save all open files before a build. There are also some sub-branches here where you can adjust your language settings, determine your project build order (good if one project depends on another one and needs to have one built before it), manage any linked resources that are associated with the workspace, and manage the local saved files history (how long to keep them, how many saves per file to record, and how much space to reserve for the file size).

This has been a rather lengthy review of just the General options that Zend Studio for Eclipse has at its disposal. If you are looking at some of the figures included so far, you will notice that we have gone down only one of the many different braches in the preferences tree. For the sake of space and the overall purpose of this book, we are skipping over all the other main tree branches and now focusing only on the PHP preferences branch.

PHP Preferences

Under the PHP branch, as the preference's name suggests, you adjust and maintain the options available to you in Zend Studio for Eclipse that directly affect the PHP portion of the environment. There is a lot to be done and a great deal that is within your power to control.

When you click on the PHP main branch level of the preferences, you see an option on what will happen when you double-click on something in the PHP Explorer. You can either have Zend Studio for Eclipse go into the selected element or have the element expanded if that is possible. If you have the Link with Editor option also turned on in the IDE, you see duplicating actions because the link activates on the first click of the mouse and then the double-click action takes place.

Code Analyzer

The second major section in the PHP preferences branch is labeled Code Analyzer. Here, you can control the severity levels of the anything that the analyzer picks up and give them one of three levels: error, warning, or ignore. You can even do this on a project-by-project basis. The code analyzer scans through your open code as you create it or as you import or modify existing code. Any issues that it comes upon are reported in the Problems view and are also displayed in the code editor as errors (in red usually) or warnings (in yellow). The option here is to be able to turn off certain errors that may occur repeatedly or raise lighter issues to full-scale error codes; it is up to you and you can define each code issue to be different.

Code Coverage

The Code Coverage portion of the PHP preferences area is merely a representation of what will be displayed when you run the code profiler. The code that has been covered is shown with different shading than code that has not been covered. The colors that can be used are available in the General Preferences section; locate Appearance, Colors and Fonts, and then expand the PHP Debug Tree option.

Code Gallery

Code Gallery is the next section available to you for control and management. Here, you can select from your own code library of classes or functions and one supplied online by Zend. You can also include others that may exist by using the Add functionality. After these galleries are activated within your copy of Zend Studio for Eclipse, you can choose code from within them for use in your own projects.

Debug

Because a large part of Zend's fame is based on its rock-solid PHP debugger technology, you would expect a lot of options in the Debug portion for you to manage. This is indeed the case with the Debug options under the PHP branch within Zend Studio for Eclipse. Figure 3.9 shows the main level of the debugger preferences. Here, you can select the default server that you want to run the debugger through and what version of PHP you will be debugging within.

Within the PHP Debug branch are two sub-branches labeled Installed Debuggers and Workbench Options. Within the Installed Debuggers branch you can manage the finer details of the debugger that is in use by selecting it and clicking on Configure. There you can change the Debug Port, the client Host/IP number and a few other options. If you had a different debugger definition installed here, this is the place that you would adjust its settings as well.

Under the branch called Workbench Options you can make some choices about how the debugger will react when it is invoked. You can tell Zend Studio for Eclipse to revert to the PHP perspective when the debugger is finished and you can allow multiple debug sessions to run concurrently just to name the first two.

Editor

Moving on from the Debug options, we next go to the Editor options branch. These options are specific to the editing of PHP code. Other, more general editor options are controlled under the General Preferences branch discussed earlier in this chapter.

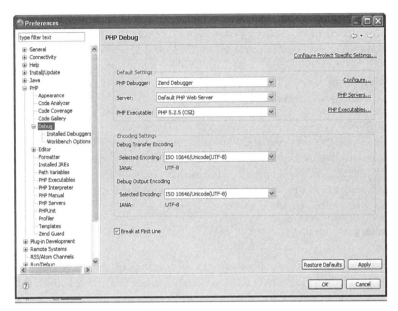

Figure 3.9   The main PHP Debug page of the Preferences window.

Code Assist

In the Code Assist section of the Editor preferences, you can control how and when the code promptings of PHP are activated. As you can see in Figure 3.10, there are a number of items that you can control. Interesting to note here is the fact that the code assistant is context sensitive. When you are in a code file and there are variables defined in other classes or functions within the same file, they are not, by default, offered within the Code Assist pop-up.

Other options here control other aspects of Code Assist. The biggest option is the one that directs Zend Studio for Eclipse to either overwrite on the insertion of code or insert the completed code. Insertion is the default choice.

Last on this screen is the enabling or disabling of the auto-activation of the code assist itself, and if the auto activation is enabled, how long in milliseconds to delay before the code assistant pops up.

You can also do some filtering within the list of code that is offered during the assist listing of possible hits. You can screen out constants, make the constants' inclusion be case sensitive, and so on. At the bottom of this window is the control of how the code assistant is launched (automatically and with or without a timer delay). Figure 3.11 shows the code assistant activated when one of the session functions is being coded.

Notice that this code assistant is also available for the PHPDoc portion of your coding. When the PHPDoc borders are defined properly (/**), you can start typing in any of the predefined attributes (@author, @return, @Desc, and so on) of the block, and the code assistant begins to help you right away.

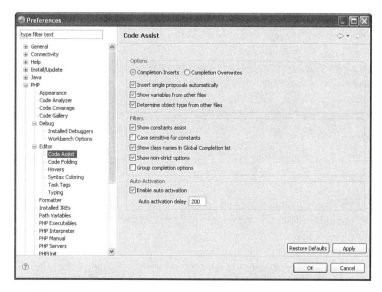

Figure 3.10   The Code Assist page of the Preferences window.

Figure 3.11   PHP code assistant in action.

Folding

Code folding is the next option available to you as you travel down the Editor preferences branch. Code folding is the ability to suppress the code that is grouped together in a function or class methods. The benefit is to collapse any code that you are working on that you know is functioning properly because you simply want it out of the way for now. The preferences here are few, in that you can turn the folding feature on or off and that you can initially fold classes, functions, or PHPDoc portions of code. HTML code can also be folded in the code editor, but there are currently no preference features with which to control it.

Hovers

Next on the list of preferences within your domain of control in Zend Studio for Eclipse is the ability to manipulate the hovering effect within the PHP code editor. If you pause (hover) your mouse pointer over a function definition, for example, you see a pop-up box that describes the full definition of that function. And if you press the Control (Ctrl) button at the same time as you hover, you see the full code definition of that function.

Syntax Coloring

Syntax coloring is a great feature for PHP developers. The features within your control are those of the coloring of the code within its contexts. This is more simply known as the *content types*, and they are all listed in the control box at the top of this window. The PHP tags themselves (Boundary Maker), the HEREDOC designation, the variables, and so on are all colored differently within the code editor. As you can see in Figure 3.12, the comments are bold and italicized.

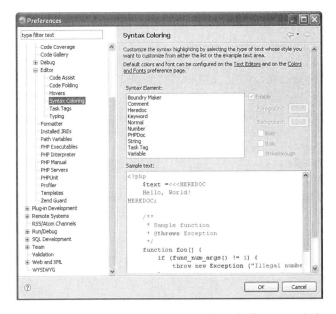

Figure 3.12   The Syntax Coloring page of the Preferences window.

If you ever get into trouble with the code colorizations, you can either restore the default settings for the content type in question or restore the default settings for all the content types by choosing the appropriate button at the bottom of this window.

Task Tags

The task tags are the next items within the Editor preferences that are at your disposal to manage. They are the different designations that you can set up within the Task Manager view. They are the different tags that you assign to the different tasks that may need attention within your projects. You can make them High, Normal, or Low in priority. As shown in Figure 3.13, three task tags are defined in the Preferences window, and all three of them are in use in the code editor and listed in the Tasks view just below that. Additionally, you can see in the code editor that these task tags are activated only within the context of code comments.

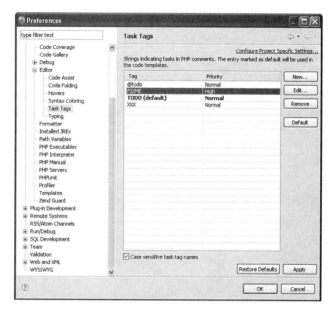

Figure 3.13   The Task Tags page of the Preferences
window and tags in use in PHP code editor.

Typing

In the next section, called Typing, you are able to control how certain parts of your code can be automatically completed for you. For example, when you begin to code a function and are beginning to open the curly braces, you can have Zend Studio for Eclipse automatically close the braces for you. This feature can be a great convenience, or it can be an annoyance. If you want to enter some other text and are not yet ready to close the brace, you spend just as much time removing the offered closing brace as you would save by having it done for you. On the other hand, how often have you been looking at your code wondering where the syntax error is, just to discover that you did not close an open brace?

Your decision whether to turn on this feature comes down to what you are used to and what you want Zend Studio for Eclipse to do for you. The other items that can be automatically completed for you are strings, round braces, square brackets, and PHPDoc comment regions. You can also control how the Tab key works within the coding context from this dialog.

Formatter

Formatter is next on the list. Specific to the PHP portion of Zend Studio for Eclipse is how the code is indented and formatted when you run the code formatter within the code editor. You can write your code as ugly as you like and then run the code formatter on the open file, and it will perform its cleanup formatting on the code based on your settings here (see Figure 3.14).

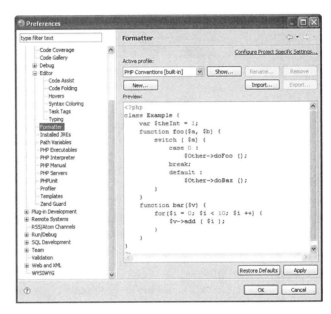

Figure 3.14   Display of selected formatting profile.

What you initially see in this dialog is merely a sample of what your code will look like after it is run through the formatter. To alter the appearance, you need to select the format profile from the drop-down list at the top and then click on Show. In the resulting tabbed dialog, shown in Figure 3.15, you have total control of how your braces are indented, if your braces should be on the same line as the defining entity, where you want whitespace, and quite a lot more. When your changes are ready, just save them, and you return to the displaying dialog to see what it will all look like.

You can even define your own code formatting profile by clicking on the New button and using an already-defined profile as a starting point. You also have to name your new profile before you can begin altering your settings. And, as is true for many of these preference settings, you can also make a formatting profile on a project-level basis by using the link at the top right of this dialog.

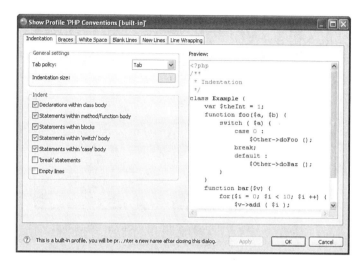

Figure 3.15   Formatting profile creation dialog.

All the above subsections in the Editor preferences area are merely directives that tell Zend Studio for Eclipse where these features are located. With a few exceptions, these items are simply told where (what path) their information or functionality lies. For example, the PHP Executables option just needs a name for the executable in question and its path location.

Skipping a few of the other minor branch options entirely, we will next touch on a few of the remaining less significant ones to make you aware of them and to briefly comment on their functionality.

Profiler

The Profiler option merely wants to know if it should automatically switch to the profile perspective when you start a profiling session. You can have it start, not start, or ask you each time.

Templates

The Templates option provides another great potential time-saver for PHP developers. The code templates section allows you to set up code frameworks or skeletons and incorporate them into your code as you write by using a simple keyboard combination. When these templates are built, they are invoked in concert with the code assist process.

If you are writing a lot of code, for example, that often uses an `ifthen` construct, you can set up a template called ifthen and define the skeleton of the code there, as shown in Figure 3.16. You can even insert standard values like a reference to today's date and where you want the cursor to land after the block of code is inserted into the PHP editor.

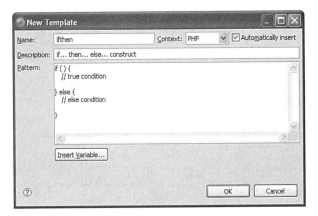

Figure 3.16   Defining an ifthen code template and
assigning it a key combination.

To call these templates after they are defined, begin to type their name, and you see that
name offered to you in the code assistant. When you have it in focus, press Enter to
select that template, and it is inserted into your editor at the current location of the
cursor.

These templates can also be imported and exported so that other developers or team
members who are interested in your templates can use them.

Summary

This chapter really only scratched the proverbial surface of how you can manipulate
Zend Studio for Eclipse to be a totally customizable Integrated Development
Environment. We hope we have shown you enough information in this area of Zend
Studio for Eclipse that you now feel comfortable with changing some of these features
and controls yourself. Don't be afraid to experiment with these features either, because
there is quite often a way provided that will bring you back to the starting point.

4

The Code Editor

The Zend Studio for Eclipse code editor is the location or view in which you will spend the majority of your development time. Therefore, it is important that you really get to know what its potential is and just how much power is stored within it. This chapter focuses exclusively on the code editor and what it can do in the theme of code development. This chapter does not cover the debugging features; Chapters 11, "Introduction to Debugging", and 12, "Running/Stepping Through Your Code", are devoted to that aspect of the editor and its extensions into other views.

Let's first look at Figure 4.1, which shows the code editor, and then look at the features that are pointed out on it.

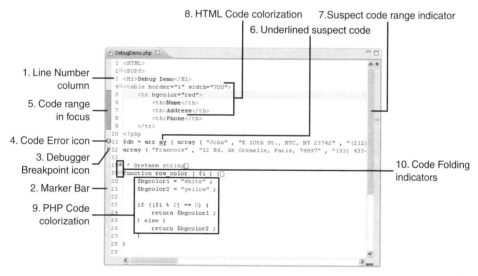

Figure 4.1   PHP code editor with important sections pointed out.

Now let's go over the areas that are pointed out in detail in the order they are numbered:

1. This is the line number column of the code editor. When errors are reported, every attempt is made to locate the line number that the event occurred on; this is your reference for locating and resolving the problem. You can turn these line numbers on and off in Zend Studio for Eclipse preferences.

2. This is the marker bar. It is the gray left margin that displays any contextual information to the code. Error and warning icons, debugger breakpoints, and code ranges are all displayed here.

3. This is a debugger breakpoint icon. You can turn this feature on and off on a line-by-line basis and can control it by right-clicking on the line in question within the marker bar and selecting Toggle Breakpoints. You can also accomplish this by double-clicking on the line in question within the marker bar to turn on or off the breakpoint.

4. This is a code error icon. It is displayed when Zend Studio for Eclipse finds something that is a fatal error in the code. A yellow triangle caution sign appears if there is just a warning situation to report. If the error is not immediately apparent (in this case, the `array` keyword is broken in two), hover the mouse pointer over the error icon in the marker bar to get more information on the error.

5. This is the representation of the code range currently in focus within the code editor. The long blue band shows up in the marker bar to show the range of the context. In this case it shows the range of code between the `<tr>` and `</tr>` tags. This feature is helpful if you have many embedded tags and want to see the start and end of a particular range.

6. When the code editor finds some code that is in question, it underlines the errant code with a red squiggly line. Shown here, the code editor has detected that the code `ay` (broken array function call) is wrong.

7. On the far right side of the code editor is another representation of discovered code errors. The red box in the right margin indicates a general location in the code where errors reside.

8. HTML code highlighting is shown in this item. Here, the HTML is colorized (you are able to customize the colors in the preferences). In the current context the HTML tags are one color, the options within the tags are another color, and the raw text is yet another color.

9. The PHP code is also colorized and also customizable. Here, variable names appear in one color, their assigned values appear in another color, language constructs appear in still another color, and so on.

10. Included within the line numbers column is also the capability to fold down sections of code that are not required for viewing at any moment in time. Here, you see the code from lines 19 to 23 folded down and represented by the gray plus sign icon. To expand the folded code, click on the plus sign; the code is expanded, and the icon is changed to a minus sign.

PHP Code Assist

The code assistant is a great tool to help you save time with code development by contextually suggesting completed code for you. By *contextually*, I mean that the code editor "knows" where you are in your code (writing HTML or PHP) and can suggest completed code accordingly.

In Figure 4.2, the section of code being written is calling the `array` function. At the placement of the cursor (as the code word `array` is being keyed in), the code assistant is activated within a pop-up overlay with all possible suggestions that it is aware of.

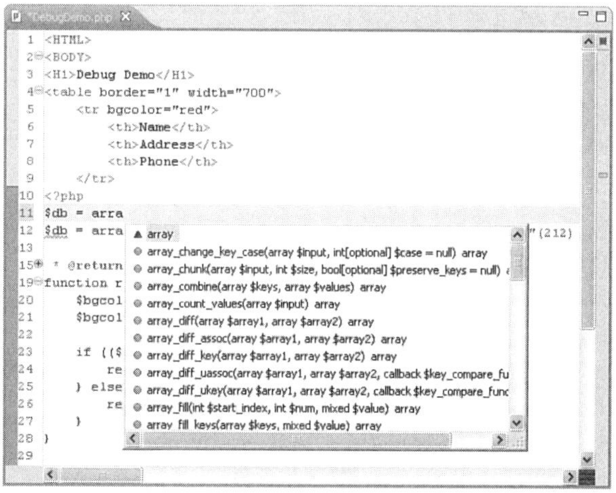

Figure 4.2   The PHP code editor with the code assistant pop-up shown.

As you can see, there are a lot of code particles that have to do with arrays. You can scroll down this list and select the function that you want by pressing Enter on the correct line or by double-clicking on the same. When the item that you want is finally selected, the code assistant inserts the code portion that you want and places the cursor at the best possible location.

If you have code templates defined, they are also included in the list of offered code completion items. If they are selected, the same process takes place, except that you may be inserting a number of code lines rather than completing a single code function command.

Another aspect of the code assistant is that if you are entering a function call that has parameters defined for it, it takes you through the completion of the function's syntax for you. As you can see in Figure 4.3, we are in the middle of completing a function call to a MySQL database-related function and are working on the second expected parameter.

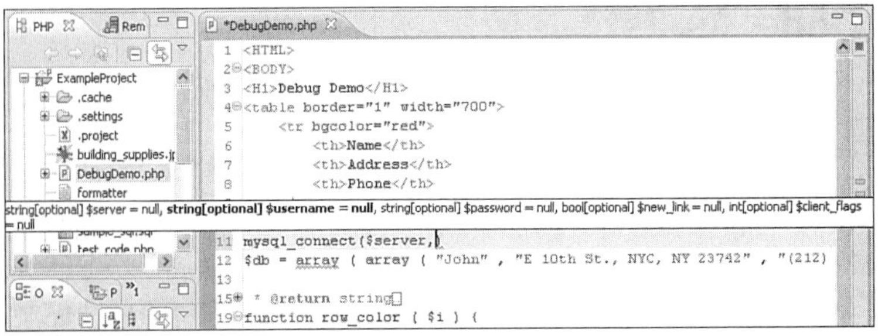

Figure 4.3   The PHP code editor with the code
assistant helping on function parameters.

The preferences to the code assistant feature are available under that PHP section, which you open by selecting Window, Preferences. There is some detailed explanation of the options in Chapter 3, "Environmental Settings."

Code Formatter

The next feature that we want to look at in this chapter is the code formatter. This feature was covered briefly in Chapter 3.

Using the code in Figure 4.4 as an example, two segments of code are not formatted well for readability. The first one is an HTML segment showing a <tr> tag and some <th> tags all aligned to the left side of the code editor. Then further down into the PHP code is an if statement that is likewise left-aligned.

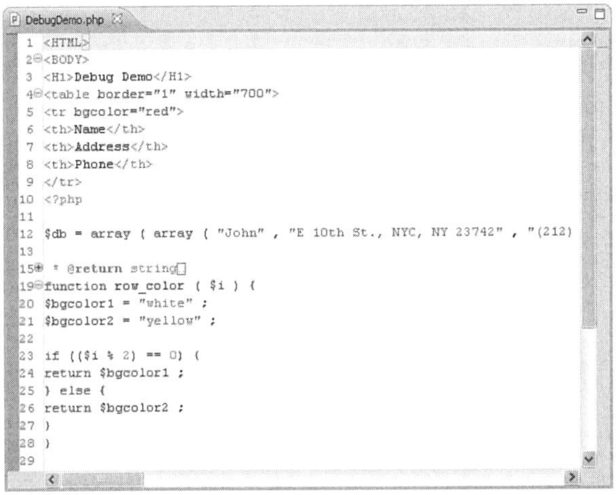

Figure 4.4   Code in poor format for both HTML and PHP.

Right-clicking on the code editor opens a pop-up menu with a Format option. After you choose this option, the code formatter then goes through the code file in question and formats it using the rules that you have established in the Zend Studio for Eclipse HTML preferences (for HTML code) and Zend Studio for Eclipse PHP preferences (for PHP code). You can select Format Active Elements if you want to format only a selected section of code; otherwise, the Format menu item involves the entire open code file. Figure 4.5 shows the properly formatted file after the code formatter has done its job.

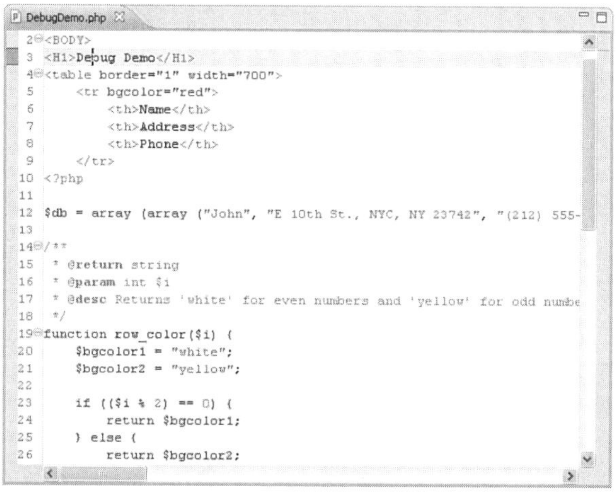

Figure 4.5   Code in proper format for both HTML and PHP.

Properties View

The last item to look at in relation to the code editor is the Properties view. You display this view by selecting Window, Show View, Other, and selecting the view by this name from the General folder. As you can see in Figure 4.6, this view is much like a Properties screen that you can see in any client/server-style IDE.

There are some neat features to this view that, at the time of this writing, are activated only for the HTML portion of the code editor. As you can see in this example, all the attributes for the HTML table tag are displayed in a grid format. This is a fully editable view, and the nice thing about it is that it is bidirectional. By this, I mean that as you write HTML code, this view updates itself with any changes as they are typed. It also works in the other direction in that if you make adjustments in the grid, it also updates the code automatically.

There is more coverage of the Properties view in Chapter 14, "The WYSIWYG Designer."

Figure 4.6   Properties view with `<table>` tag in focus.

Summary

You were given a good introduction to the PHP code editor in this chapter. A few other gems can be found or launched from within this code editor, such as the debug process and refactoring process. These features are well covered in other areas of this book, and you are also sure to find some of these features on your own as you become more proficient with this code editor.

Views in the PHP Perspective

We have already talked about perspectives and how using different perspectives for different tasks can improve productivity. If you want to know more about perspectives, be sure to read Chapter 3, "Environmental Settings." This chapter focuses specifically on the PHP perspective.

In this chapter we take a closer look at five important views: Outline, PHP Project Outline, PHP Functions, Problems, and Tasks views. They are some of the default views in the PHP perspective. If you have changed the locations of default views in your window, they may appear in different places on your screen.

Getting Started

To help us with the examination of views, we need some sample code. Functions, classes, variables, errors, and tasks will show up in the view windows. We are going to make a simple Number class later in this chapter to showcase several features. Before we do that, let's get some basic information on each of the views; then we can see how they work together in the bigger scheme of things.

Outline View

The Outline view breaks all elements in a selected file into an easy-to-read format. If you have a new project with a new PHP file in it, when you declare a function or class, it appears in the Outline view. As a file gets more complex, this view becomes more useful.

The Outline view uses icons to represent different elements in code. A class is represented by a large circle with a C in the middle of it. Public variables that belong to a class are represented by a hollow circle, whereas private variables are represented by a hollow square. Finally, functions, whether they belong to a class or are independent, are represented by a solid circle. Look at Figure 5.1 to see how the Outline view represents code elements from a file.

Figure 5.1   Variables and functions in the Outline view.

PHP Project Outline View

If you switch to the PHP Project Outline view, you see similar information to the Outline view. For some files and projects, this information is actually identical. As you build more complexity into a project, these views will start to hold different information. We go over exactly what the differences are when we start to write some code.

The PHP Project view is a good way to get a quick overview of a project. Some of the other views that we are going to discuss, such as the Problems and Tasks views, display information for all opened projects. The PHP Project Outline view shows information only for the selected project. This is a logical way to display information, but it is something that is important to keep in mind if you are working on several projects at once.

In Figure 5.2, notice that classes, variables, and functions are represented in the PHP Project view by the same symbols as are used in the Outline view.

PHP Functions View

The PHP Functions view is an extremely useful feature of Zend Studio for Eclipse. If you constantly find yourself on the php.net website, you will get a lot of use out of this view. It is basically an outline view of the PHP manual at your fingertips. You can pull up the website manual page directly in Zend Studio for Eclipse if you need to read more about a function by right-clicking on it and clicking Open Manual. Double-clicking on a function inserts it into your code at the position of the cursor.

The list in the PHP Functions view is organized by PHP constants, PHP classes or modules that come with a standard install of PHP, and then the regular functions that are familiar to most programmers. The nice thing about the list in this view is that it is exhaustive. Virtually anything that you might want more information on is included in this window. The list is long, but it is organized in a logical way and finding things is not difficult. As you can see from Figure 5.3, there is a lot to look through in this view.

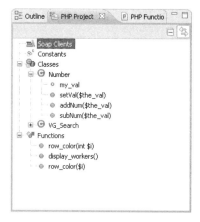

Figure 5.2   Expanded components of the PHP Project Outline view.

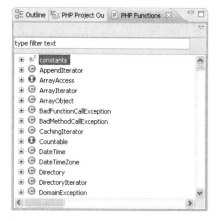

Figure 5.3   List of functions in the PHP Functions view.

Problems View

The Problems view appears by default at the bottom of the screen, under the code editor. This view delivers useful information about errors and warnings in your code but is updated only after files have been saved. As you might expect, double-clicking on an error or warning takes you to the line of code that is responsible.

The Problems view shows all problems (errors, warnings, or infos) for all files in all opened projects. For the simplest debugging, make sure that you have only one project open at a time. However, in certain cases, simultaneous debugging of multiple projects might come in handy.

Although the Problems view displays errors, warnings, and infos, it shows only information about the most serious until that category in a given file has been fixed. That means you could have a dozen warnings (for example, printing a variable before a value has been assigned to it) and only one error, and only the error would show up in the Problems view. The warnings are hidden until the error is fixed.

Figure 5.4 shows a project with errors and warnings in two different files. Notice that the filename where the error exists is shown in the Resource column of the Problems view, and that the files in the PHP Explorer view have error or warning icons next to them.

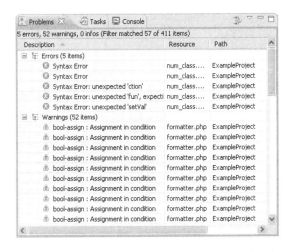

Figure 5.4   Errors and warnings across two files in the Problems view.

Tasks View

The Tasks view is an extremely useful feature. It makes use of certain types of comments left in code and turns them into a task or communication system that could be used by a single programmer or a group. Double-clicking on a task takes you to the file and the line where the comment was typed. The Tasks view also gives you a checkbox that can be used to mark completed tasks.

The default way to enter a task is to type **//TODO** anywhere in your code. Anything typed after TODO on the same line is added to the description of the task. This is fine, but what if you want to really make use of the task system and have different types of tasks with different priorities? You can set up your own task options by opening the Zend Studio for Eclipse Preferences window (Window, Preferences) and then select PHP, Editor, Task Tags. You could create a new task tag called HOTFIX and set the priority of this type of task to High. After you create the tag, typing **//HOTFIX** anywhere in your code creates a HOTFIX task and marks it as High priority.

Remember that the Tasks view shows tasks for all projects that are opened in the PHP Explorer. If you have several projects opened, each with several tasks outstanding, the log could get quite full. The Tasks view can be as complicated or as simple as you choose to make it. Figure 5.5 shows a simple example of how tasks may be used in a project.

Figure 5.5   Creating a task in code and displaying it in the Tasks View.

We are done with our overview of views, but before we move on, let's look at how to move views around, close them, and restore them. Not many things are more frustrating than finally getting comfortable with a piece of software and then accidentally closing or moving something and not being able to get it back the way it was.

You may have discovered that you can click and drag views around and even close them completely. This is a useful feature that allows you to work in a workspace that you have complete control over. On the chance that you close a view by clicking on the X or you move a view and then forget where you put it, you can select Window, Show View and then choose one of the views, or click on the Other menu item to get it back.

Filters

As we already pointed out, the Task and Problems views display all outstanding tasks or problems for all opened projects. One way to control what is displayed in these views is to close projects that you are not working on. If you find that you need to have more than one project open but still want to see only certain tasks or problems, you're in luck. You can apply filters to both the Tasks view and the Problems view.

The filters available for tasks and problems are slightly different. We look at both of them here, but we start with task filters. Click on the filter icon at the top right of the Tasks view. This brings up the Filters window, as shown in Figure 5.6.

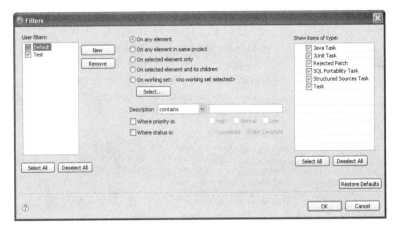

Figure 5.6   Filtering options for tasks.

In this window, you can create custom filtering profiles. Each profile can be named and have specific filters in place associated with it. Start by clicking New in the Filters window. You can name your profile and then filter tasks by elements, projects, description, priority, status, and type. Filters have a Restore Defaults option, so don't be afraid of ruining the settings.

The filter icon for problems looks the same as the one for tasks, except that you must be in the Problems view. If you click on the icon, or look at Figure 5.7, you'll notice that the Filters windows are almost identical. You can create custom filters profiles in the area on the left of the window and change the filtering preferences. The preferences available for problem filtering are specific to the Problems view and include options such as severity of the problem.

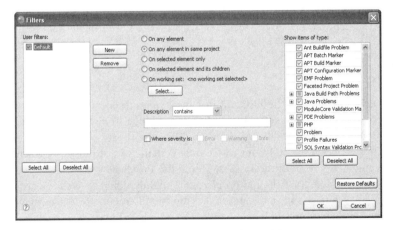

Figure 5.7   Filtering options for problems.

Views in Action

Now that you have an idea of what these views do, let's take a closer look at them in a more realistic light. As you add functions and classes, include external files, define constants, and make notes to yourself or other developers, these views begin to become more interesting. Let's take a closer look at the differences between the Outline view and PHP Project Outline view; then we will watch them change as we add some sample code to a project.

The main difference between the Outline and PHP Project Outline is that the Outline view shows the outline only for a single file. If your project has only one file and you have it open, these views look pretty much the same. Let's put some code in a project to illustrate the differences.

If you want to follow along with this example, open Zend Studio for Eclipse now. Create a new project called Number. To avoid confusion, close any other projects that might be open.

Start by creating a file called `num_class.php`. This will be a simple class that will model a number. It will have a value and will be able to add or subtract other numbers with its own value. Listing 5.1 shows what the class is going to look like.

Listing 5.1 `num_class.php`—**A Simple Class to Illustrate How Views Represent Code Elements**

```php
<?php

/*
 * filename: num_class.php
 *
 * This is a very simple Number class
 * Numbers will know their value and be able to add or subtract
 *
 */

class Number {

    public $my_val;

    function setal($the_val) {
        $this->my_val = $the_val;
    }

    function addNum($the_val) {
        return $this->my_val + $the_val;
    }
```

Listing 5.1   **Continued**

```
    function subNum($the_val) {
        return $this->my_val - $the_val;
    }


}


?>
```

After entering the code, take a look at the Outline view. The class that was just created has been turned into a tree structure with the class name at the top, then the variables, and then the functions. If you mouse over the functions, the tool tip shows you what arguments can be passed to the function and what is returned.

Click on the PHP Project Outline view to see a different presentation of information. At this point, the Outline and PHP Project Outline views look similar. The difference is the way the information is categorized. The only heading that has any information at this point is the `classes` heading. It should show you exactly the same information that was previously in the Outline view. There are no Soap clients or defined constants yet, so these headings have nothing under them. You might wonder why the `functions` heading is empty because we did define three functions. This heading displays only functions that are not attached to a class. The functions that we wrote appear under the `Number` class and are not repeated.

Let's see what happens to these views with a few more files. We need a file that will make use of the class. We can call it `driver.php`. Listing 5.2 shows what it looks like.

Listing 5.2   `driver.php`—**A Runnable File That Makes Use of the** `Number` **Class**

```php
<?php

/*
 * filename: driver.php
 *
 * Run the number class
 *
 */

require_once('num_class.php');

define('ONE', 1);

$num_one = new Number;
$num_one->seta1(5);
echo $num_one->addNum(ONE);


?>
```

If you look at the Outline view, you will notice that it is quite different from the Outline view for `num_class.php`. You should see an entry in the outline for the included file (`num_class.php`) and the defined constant (`ONE`). This view is a powerful tool for visualizing relationships among multiple files at a glance.

Take another look at the PHP Project Outline view with the new file. The only difference should be that there is something in the `constants` heading now. You might notice that the included file does not show up in this view. The reason is that included files do not make that much sense when you are thinking of the project as a whole. This is where the differences between these views start to become evident. We take a closer and more detailed look at these views in the second half of this book when we build a usable application.

Summary

After reading this chapter, you should have an idea of how to use the Outline, PHP Outline, PHP Functions, Problems, and Tasks views. You do not have to be an expert on these views to be able to create a project in Zend Studio for Eclipse. However, becoming comfortable with them will increase your productivity and help you identify relationships or problems in your code.

Code Gallery

Code reuse is an important part of many programmers' lives. Most people understand the benefits of code reuse, but anyone who has had to search through hundreds of files for that "snippet that does exactly what you are trying to do" understands the need for some kind of organization or directory feature for code. Besides you just being able to find the code that you are looking for, unless the code is trivial, there is probably some code in a reused snippet that has to be modified every time you use it.

Zend Studio for Eclipse comes with a full-featured code gallery. It has two major types of galleries that should make development significantly easier and faster as the code gallery grows. The first type of gallery is the user (or local) gallery. This gallery is limited to use only by a single user on his or her installation of Zend Studio for Eclipse. The second type of gallery is the gallery maintained by Zend for Zend Studio for Eclipse code snippets. Zend Studio users may already be familiar with this.

User Code Gallery

The user galleries and Zend galleries are accessed in similar ways. There are just a few extra steps to connect to the nonlocal ones. Let's start by looking at the simplest case first. To start with, you have to find the Code Gallery view. You can open it by selecting Window, Show View, Code Gallery or by using the fast view selector at the bottom left of your screen. Figure 6.1 shows the Code Gallery tree view as well as the icons used to interact with your galleries.

The Code Gallery view allows you to synchronize your gallery with a nonlocal repository; configure your gallery options (connections); and add, edit, or delete snippets. We look at the synchronization and configuration in the following sections. Right now, let's start by creating a code snippet.

Click on the New Entry button in the Code Gallery view. This opens a new window that will hold information about the code snippet that you are adding. You must name the snippet, include the author information, and, of course, add the code snippet. You may also include a short description about what the code snippet does. Figure 6.2 shows the code snippet creation window.

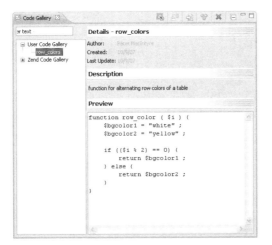

Figure 6.1   The Code Gallery view.

Figure 6.2   Creating a simple code snippet.

After you have added a snippet to your gallery, you can search through the available snippets by expanding the tree on the left column of the Code Gallery view, or you can narrow down the results by typing the first few letters of the snippet name. Add the snippet to your code by clicking on the Insert button. This adds the selected snippet at the position of your cursor in a file. If you have no files open, the snippet is not added anywhere.

Snippets in the user gallery can be edited or deleted. Use the icons at the top of the gallery window, or right-click on a snippet and select Edit or Delete.

We mentioned earlier that you could suggest that your code snippets should be added to the Zend gallery. You can do this by choosing the Suggest option on a particular snippet. All you need is a free Zend.com user account. You are asked which gallery you want to suggest the snippet to and what category it should be added to.

Zend Gallery

The Zend gallery is an online code gallery that is maintained by Zend. Code snippets in this gallery come from several sources. Some are added by programmers at Zend, but many are added by Zend Studio for Eclipse users. These snippets are added to the main Zend gallery by "suggestions." You can suggest code by right-clicking on a code snippet and choosing the Suggest option.

You can connect to the Zend code gallery in the Code Gallery view. A Zend.com user account is all you need to connect to the gallery and browse useful code snippets. Besides the user Zend galleries, you can connect to other remote galleries by adding a new gallery by URL in the Preferences window. See Figure 6.3 for a better look at adding a new code gallery.

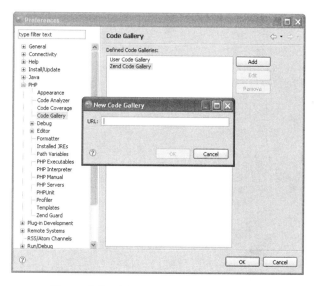

Figure 6.3   Adding a code gallery by URL.

Summary

The code gallery in Zend Studio for Eclipse can be used in two main ways. Individual programmers can maintain a local repository of snippets for personal use. They can also connect and contribute to the Zend repository online, which can be accessed via Zend Studio for Eclipse.

Code Analyzer

Zend Studio for Eclipse includes some powerful and customizable features for code analysis. Your first question might be, "What is a code analyzer?" The answer is, "A bunch of things." More formally, a *code analyzer* is a suite of tools that provide visual and interactive ways to write, debug, and maintain code. This chapter outlines ways that you can use and configure the code analyzer for your projects.

The code analyzer uses visual cues in the code editor and the Problems view. These cues include highlighting and underlining code and placing icons in the margins of the code editor. Tool tips are also available to provide further information about errors and warnings. Let's begin by looking at how the code analyzer can be configured.

Configuring the Code Analyzer

As with most things in Zend Studio for Eclipse, the default settings for the code analyzer work fine for most users and most tasks. However, when the need to change a configuration setting arises, not knowing how to make the change can be frustrating. To avoid future frustration, let's look at the configuration window.

Select Window, Preferences; then find PHP in the Preferences tree, and click on the Code Analyzer branch. The window that you should see now is shown in Figure 7.1.

Each heading in this window gives a description of something that the code analyzer is monitoring with a drop-down that tells Zend Studio for Eclipse how to treat that case. You can choose to treat cases as errors, warnings, or ignore them completely. Some cases allow only the selection of warning or ignore.

What this feature allows you to do is change the feedback that is shown to you while developing on a granular scale. For example, by default, the use of a variable before it has been defined will generate a warning. However, you can set the severity of this particular situation so that it causes an error instead, or you may choose to ignore the warnings. For a complete list of configuration options, see Table 7.1. Default settings are in bold.

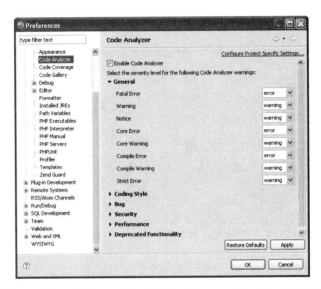

Figure 7.1   Options in the Code Analyzer configuration window.

Table 7.1   **Code Analyzer Configuration Options**

Type of Error	Severity of Warning
General	
Fatal Error	**Error** | Warning | Ignore
Warning	Error | **Warning** | Ignore
Notice	Error | **Warning** | Ignore
Core Error	**Error** | Warning | Ignore
Core Warning	Error | **Warning** | Ignore
Compile Error	**Error** | Warning | Ignore
Compile Warning	Error | **Warning** | Ignore
Strict Error	**Error** | Warning | Ignore
Coding Style	
Not enough arguments for define()	**Warning** | Ignore
Use of variable before definition	**Warning** | Ignore
Bug	
Possibly problematic one-line comment	**Warning** | Ignore
Assignment in condition	**Warning** | Ignore
Result of print/echo used as Boolean	**Warning** | Ignore
Object used as Boolean	**Warning** | Ignore
If-if-else without block parentheses	**Warning** | Ignore

Table 7.1   **Continued**

Type of Error	Severity of Warning
First argument for define() is not a string	**Warning** | Ignore
Break with variable	**Warning** | Ignore
Wrong break depth	**Warning** | Ignore
Variable name appears only once	**Warning** | Ignore
Unused function parameter	**Warning** | Ignore
Unused global declaration	**Warning** | Ignore
Using $HTTP globals in functions without defining them as global	**Warning** | Ignore
Value never used	**Warning** | Ignore
Both empty return and return with value used in function	**Warning** | Ignore
Function does not return a value but its return value is used	**Warning** | Ignore
Returning by ref but not assigning by ref	**Warning** | Ignore
Control reaches end of function but return value is used	**Warning** | Ignore
Sprintf is missing arguments	**Warning** | Ignore
Sprintf has more arguments than needed	**Warning** | Ignore
Unreachable code	**Warning** | Ignore
Variable used as object but has different type	**Warning** | Ignore
Bad escape sequence: \z, did you mean \\z?	**Warning** | Ignore
Condition without a body	**Warning** | Ignore
Expression result never used	**Warning** | Ignore
Security	
Use of global variable before definition	**Warning** | Ignore
Include() statement using variable	**Warning** | Ignore
Performance	
Passing var by reference but not modifying it	**Warning** | Ignore
Deprecated Functionality	
Use of deprecated call-time pass-by-reference	**Warning** | Ignore

After configuring the code analyzer, click Apply and then OK. You can modify the settings at any time as you get comfortable with them or as the particular needs of your project change. If you ever mess things up so badly that you need to start over, you can use the Restore Defaults button to get back on track. Note that none of the changes take effect, including restoring the default settings, until you commit the changes by clicking Apply or OK, and clicking Yes on the confirmation window (see Figure 7.2).

Figure 7.2   You have to confirm code analyzer
changes before they take effect.

Using the Code Analyzer

The code analyzer uses visual cues to deliver useful information to users. Besides displaying errors and warnings in the Problems view, the code analyzer includes icons, in-code
underlines, and colors that give information about the state of a file to the user at a
glance. Zend Studio for Eclipse uses intuitive colors to represent the severity of warnings
and errors—yellow and red, respectively. These colors apply to the underlines, icons, and
a quick-glance information square at the top-right corner of the code editor. Hovering
over this square gives you a summary of errors or warnings in a particular file. Recall
from Chapter 5, "Views in the PHP Perspective," that errors take precedence over warnings in terms of what is displayed to the user. If you have five warnings and a single
error, only the error is displayed until it is fixed.

Along with in-code underlines to highlight errors and warnings, tool tips are available
if you hover over an underlined section of code. The initial tool tip gives some general
information on the error or warning. If you remain hovering over the error and press
F2, a new window appears with a detailed description, explanation, and examples if they
are available. These tips tend to contain more useful information for warnings because,
while errors are more severe, they are often more straightforward to fix. Figure 7.3 shows
a useful message as the result of a double warning: using a variable before it has been
defined and using a variable path in an include function.

The information in the pop-up box explains that using a variable before it has been
defined is a security risk, and using a variable as the basis for an included file can also be
a security risk. It gives examples of ways that includes can be handled poorly, as well as
ways that they should be handled safely. Using this feature should help to make your
code more secure.

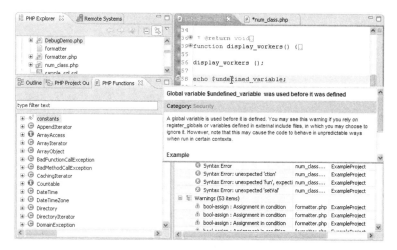

Figure 7.3   Detailed information tool tip obtained by
pressing F2 while hovering over a warning in code.

Summary

This chapter should give you a solid idea of tools available to you when you are analyzing code. Error checking is important because your code probably will not work if there
is an error in it. The warnings in Zend Studio for Eclipse are equally as valuable because
the explanations of warnings can help you write better, more secure code. The code analyzer is very configurable, and you can use all the options to customize your development environment so that you see only what you are interested in displayed in your
code editor and Problems views.

8

Refactoring

The first question that you may be asking after reading the title of this chapter is, "What is *refactoring*?" Some people may have used refactoring previously under a different name such as *projectwide renaming*. If you have used this feature before in other development tools, you will be glad to see it in Zend Studio for Eclipse, and if you have never used it before, you will probably learn to love it.

The requirements for refactoring in Zend Studio for Eclipse specify several different ways that the feature works. Those requirements are

- Rename local variables.
- Rename global variables.
- Rename data members.
- Rename methods, functions, and classes.
- Move files and folders.
- Organize imports.

In the remainder of this chapter, we examine each of these requirements and give examples of how to use them in a project.

Rename Local Variables

At first, some of the requirements for renaming appear trivial. Renaming local variables seems as though it should be straightforward, and is for the most part, except for a few cases. Let's start off with defining what we mean by "local" variables.

Local variables can be broken into two main subcategories:

- **Naïve**—The variable is not preceded by the keyword `global` and is not a super-global, and there is not a `require` statement inside the function, preceding the variable usage.

- **Advanced**—The variable is not preceded by the keyword `global` and is not a super-global, and there is a `require` statement inside the function, preceding the variable usage, but this `require` does not define a global variable with the same name.

Let's look at some examples of local variable renaming. Listing 8.1 shows a simple example of how refactoring works. If you highlight the variable $a and then select Refactor, Rename from the menu at the top of the screen, or right-click on the code editor, you see the refactoring window, as shown in Figure 8.1.

Listing 8.1   **Rename All Occurrences of** $a

```php
<?php

function foo($b) {
    $a = 4;
    $a = $a + $b;
    return $a;
}

?>
```

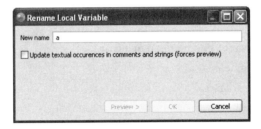

Figure 8.1   Refactoring window for variable renaming.

This window allows you to choose a new name for the selected variable. It does not allow you to preview your changes or make the changes until you have typed in a new variable name. Clicking OK applies the refactoring to the file. If you want to see what the changes are going to be like before you actually commit the changes, use the Preview option, as shown in Figure 8.2. This option must also be used to update variable names that may be in comments.

From Figure 8.2, you can see that refactoring in this simple case worked as expected. All the variables named $a were renamed to $c.

For the next example of local variable renaming, local and global variables are named the same. Although naming local and global variables the same is never a good idea, in some cases it may be necessary. It also helps to show how refactoring in Zend Studio for Eclipse works. Listing 8.2 uses the example from Listing 8.1 with a twist. Adding a global line to the code will change the outcome of the refactoring.

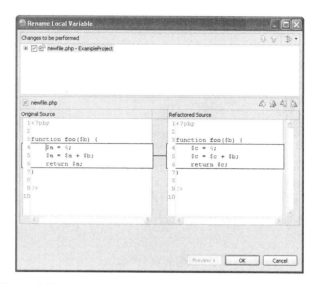

Figure 8.2   Code and comment preview window for refactoring.

Listing 8.2   **Rename All Local Occurrences of** $a

```php
<?php

function foo($b) {
    $a = 4;
    $a = $a + $b;
    global $a;
    return $a;
}

?>
```

Zend Studio for Eclipse knows the difference between local and global variables. If you highlighted the first $a in the function and renamed it to $c using refactoring, the resulting file would look like Listing 8.3. All occurrences of $a after the global statement are left unchanged.

Listing 8.3   **Result of Refactoring with Local and Global Variables**

```php
<?php

function foo($b) {
    $c = 4;
    $c = $c + $b;
```

Listing 8.3   **Continued**

```
    global $a;
    return $a;
}

?>
```

The examples that we have been looking at so far in this section have been naïve local variables. Advanced local variables are not that much more complicated than naïve variables but could yield surprising refactoring results if you were not aware of them.

Advanced local variable renaming takes care of special cases when files are included into code, and the included file(s) contains variables that are used in the parent file. Listing 8.4 shows two files with variable $a. In this case, all occurrences of the variable are renamed.

Listing 8.4   **Advanced Renaming of Local Variables**

```
<?php

// file: foo.php

function foo() {
    $a = 4;
    require('bar.php');
    return $a;
}

?>

<?php

// file: bar.php

$a = 7;

?>
```

Rename Global Variables

Renaming global variables is functionally similar to renaming local variables. However, it is good to make the logical distinction between the two types of variables because they may play a larger role in more complex code. Let's look at one simple example and one more complex example of global variable renaming.

Listing 8.5 shows a few lines of code with a mix of local and global variables. Refactoring the first occurrence of $a and naming it $c changes the first, third, and fourth occurrence of $a. The second occurrence is skipped because it is a local variable of the function foo().

Listing 8.5   **Simple Renaming of Global Variables**

```php
<?php

$a = 4;
echo foo();

function foo() {
    $c = 4;
    global $a;
    return $a;
}

?>
```

Like advanced local variable renaming, advanced global variable renaming recursively renames global variables in included files. Listing 8.6 shows an example of recursive global variable naming.

Listing 8.6   **Advanced Recursive Renaming of Global Variables**

```php
<?php

// file: foo.php

$a = 4;
require('bar.php');

?>
```

```php
<?php

// file: bar.php

$a = 7;
require ('foobar.php');

?>
```

```php
<?php
```

Listing 8.6   **Continued**

```
// file: foobar.php

$a = 16;

?>
```

All occurrences of $a in all three files can be renamed to $c by changing the first variable in the file foo.php.

Rename Data Members

Zend Studio for Eclipse is designed to rename variables inside classes and methods. Class data members are usually defined at the top of a class and then accessed using $this->*variable_name* later in methods. With refactoring, renaming data members as shown in Listing 8.7 is an easy process.

Listing 8.7   **Renaming Data Members in a Class**

```
<?php

class Foo {

    var $member_var;
    static $static_var;

    function bar() {

        echo $this->member_var;
        echo $this->static_var;

    }

}

?>
```

Both data members in the class Foo can be renamed using refactoring.

Rename Methods, Functions, and Classes

Method, function, and class names all have the possibility of changing over the development cycle of a project. As requirements evolve, it may make sense also to change function names so that they are more descriptive. Refactoring in Zend Studio for Eclipse makes these types of changes easy. Listing 8.8 shows all occurrences of a function renamed. Method and class renaming work in the same way.

Listing 8.8   **Renaming All Occurrences of a Function**

```php
<?php

// original file

function foo() {

    echo "hi";

}

foo();

?>

<?php

// refactored file

function foobar() {

    echo "hi";

}

foobar();

?>
```

Move Files and Folders

One of the most far-reaching changes that you can make to a program is a path change. Anyone who has had to make the same change in hundreds of files because the "globals" file has to be moved knows how frustrating path changes are. Let's set up a simple example to demonstrate how refactoring handles the moving of files and folders.

Suppose you have a file, we'll call it foo.php, that is calling a function in a file called lib/math_lib.php, as shown in Listing 8.9.

Listing 8.9   **Two Files to Demonstrate File Path Refactoring**

```php
<?php

// filename: foo.php

require_once('lib/math_lib.php');
```

Listing 8.9   **Continued**

```php
echo add(2,3);
?>

<?php

// filename: lib/math_lib.php

function add($num1, $num2) {
    return $num1 + $num2;
}
?>
```

Using the information from Listing 8.9, suppose that the project gets more complicated and `math_lib.php` is moved to its own directory where helper files will eventually exist. The first thing that you have to do is create the directory that the file will be moved to. To move the file to a new folder, right-click on the file that you want to move and select Refactor, Move. Next, choose the new location for the file from the window, as shown in Figure 8.3.

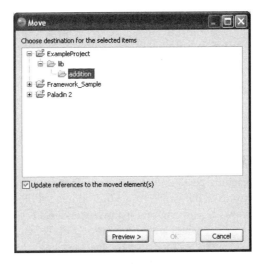

Figure 8.3   Moving a file to a new directory with refactoring.

When you are moving files, Zend Studio for Eclipse forces you to approve the move by previewing the changes that will be made in all files. After you have had a chance to look at and approve the changes, click on OK in the preview window that is shown in Figure 8.4.

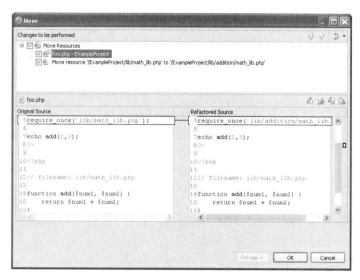

Figure 8.4   Previewing changes to code
when moving files with refactoring.

Files may have to be renamed over the course of a project. They can be renamed in the same way as they are moved. Simply select Refactor, Rename and type in a new name, and the changes are applied to all files that include that file.

Summary

Refactoring is a powerful tool. It will probably save you time at some point while you are working on a large project. Just remember that with refactoring, as with any large-scale search and replace, the results should be verified after the replacement has been done.

9

SQL Integration

Naturally, one of the major features of PHP and the dynamic Web in the past few years has been the capability to keep websites up-to-date through database integration. PHP, of course, has this capability to connect to a database, or multiple data sources, and present up-to-date content either in its "raw" format or in a "massaged" presentation. To do this, though, PHP has to establish a connection to a data source and be able to extract required or requested information.

Database Development Perspective

Naturally, Zend Studio for Eclipse has an entire perspective devoted to the management of the data source. Select the perspective titled Database Development to see this collection of views. You should see a layout similar to that shown in Figure 9.1.

As you can see just by opening this perspective, some views are open that you may not have seen previously. The Data Source Explorer view is the main view on the left side of the IDE, and you will find that you use this view the most during your work within this perspective.

Before you can use this perspective to its optimal value, you have to establish some connections to a database source. Zend Studio for Eclipse has some data sources predefined for you, and in this chapter, we use the MySQL data source. In the Data Source Explorer view, right-click on the SQL Databases item to bring up the pop-up menu. Only two items come up: New and Refresh. Click on the New item to open a connectivity dialog, entitled New JDBC Connection Profile, as shown in Figure 9.2.

Give your database connection a useful name and description for it if you want. Then decide whether you want the connection to automatically connect each time you open the Data Source Explorer. Here you will also provide your connection authorization credentials and alternately the specific name of the database you are connecting to. Be sure to test your connection here before moving forward just to be sure you are communicating to the database correctly.

Click Next to move to the last dialog in this wizard process; here, you see a summary of the connection information that you have just established. Click Finish and you are ready to use your new database interface.

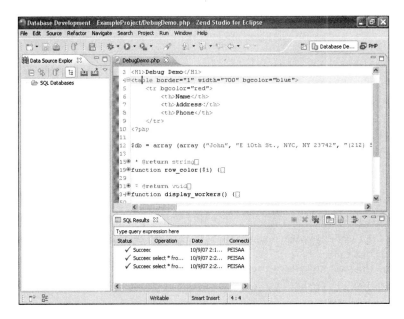

Figure 9.1   The Database Development perspective
in its initial default presentation.

Figure 9.2   New JDBC connection profile dialog.

Note

On the URL line in the New JDBC Connection Profile dialog, you may see something like `jdbc:mysql://localhost:3306/database`. If you want to connect to one specific database, then be sure to remove `database` and replace it with the name of an existing database so that it can connect to the tables.

Caution

Also be aware that sometimes if you do not specify a specific database name in the New JDBC Connection Profile, the resulting connection definition may not have any database refernces to show. So it is always better to set up each connection to a specific database.

Still in the Database Development perspective, you should now be able to drill down to your named database and look at the tables and structures defined within it, as shown in Figure 9.3.

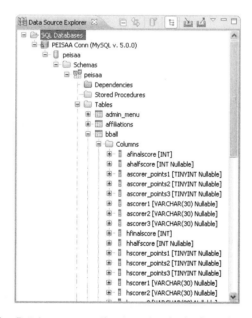

Figure 9.3   Database connection tree view in the Data Source Explorer.

Because this is a sample database being used with this book, you will, naturally, see different tables and different column names and definitions than shown here, but the overall concept is the same.

Viewing Data

Now that we have a valid and operational connection to the local database, let's draw some data out of the tables to see what that looks like.

Using the tree view to the data source just established, expand the tree to the Tables level (refer to Figure 9.3 if you need to). Right-click on any table name and select Data from the resulting pop-up menu; then select Sample Contents from the next pop-up menu. You trigger a sample SQL Select statement to be run against the table that you have chosen.

When this is done, you see an insertion into the SQL Results view (which is divided into two panes). On the left side, you see the status results of the run query, and on the right side is the SQL statement that was run and sample data that was retrieved. This window is shown in Figure 9.4. Note that you can combine the right display pane from two separate tabs into one by clicking on the toolbar item labeled Display Results in Single Tab in the toolbar at the top of the right pane. The mouse pointer is pointing to it in Figure 9.4.

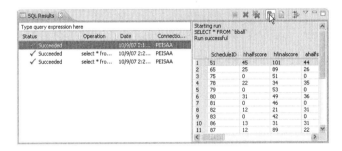

Figure 9.4   SQL Results view showing result of sample data query.

> **Note**
>
> You can adjust the columns that are displayed to you in the SQL Results view by opening the preferences for it in the SQL Results View Options (History Options) under SQL Development in the Zend Studio for Eclipse preferences area.

You can also write your own SQL queries to send to the database through your SQL connection within Zend Studio for Eclipse. This is a little different in its approach. To send SQL code to the database, you need to create a new SQL-type file so that Zend Studio for Eclipse knows that it should contain SQL code and therefore be able to handle it properly. Select File, New and then select SQL File from the next-level menu. This opens the New SQL File dialog, where you can name the file and assign it to a project (see Figure 9.5).

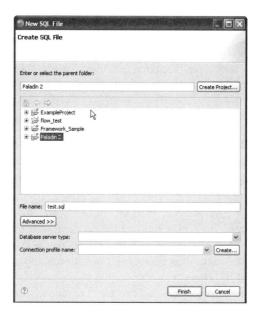

Figure 9.5   New SQL file being assigned
to a project and database source.

After you create the file, Zend Studio for Eclipse adds `sql` as a filename extension and
opens the file in the code editing section of this perspective. As you can see in Figure
9.6, you can edit and create SQL statements that are more complex than the simple data
inquiry shown in the previous section. In this figure, there is a series of drop-down lists
across the top of this code editor that display the current assigned connections to this
SQL file. If you have other connections that this SQL context can also interface with,
flexibility is added here to change those connections on the fly and run other SQL if
you so desire. After you write the SQL code that you want, you can execute it against
the current connection by pressing Ctrl+Alt+X, or if you have selected SQL in a larger
file to run, you can press the more simple Alt+X to run the code (these options also
appear on the right-click pop-up menu for you to select).

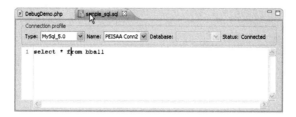

Figure 9.6   New SQL file created and open for editing.

> **Note**
>
> If you want to write and test some SQL against a table, you can use the SQL Scrapbook icon on the SQL Perspectives toolbar to quickly create an SQL editing file for you. You can make your connections from the drop-down lists that appear at the top of this file, and you are all set to run the SQL.

Data Manipulation

The data in your tables also can be edited from within this perspective. Under the Data submenu in the right-click pop-up menu, there are three other options we have not covered yet. The first is labeled Edit. When you select this option while pointing to a table, the data from that table is loaded into an Editor tab, and you are allowed to edit the contents. Keep in mind that after you edit the contents, you still have to save the changes back into the table. After you save your changes to the contents of a table, an SQL UPDATE statement is actually generated and executed against the database; this is then displayed in the SQL Results view for further scrutiny.

The other two items on the Data submenu are Load and Extract. They are basically import and export options available on a table-by-table basis.

Table Manipulations

The Database Development perspective is not limited to query execution alone. You can also delete tables and draw out the Data Definition Language (DDL) for all defined tables.

To delete an unwanted table, select that table in the Data Source Explorer, right-click, and choose Delete from the pop-up menu. This generates the drop table SQL code for you and opens it in a new code editor for you to inspect before you execute the code. Following is an example of the code generated for you:

```
ALTER TABLE admin_menu CHANGE COLUMN menuid menuid INT NOT NULL;
ALTER TABLE admin_menu DROP PRIMARY KEY;
DROP TABLE admin_menu;
```

The process to generate the DDL code for your tables is similar. Select a table, right-click, and then select Generate DDL from the pop-up menu. A dialog appears with options, as shown in Figure 9.7. Here, you can choose the generation options such as adding a DROP TABLE directive, using fully qualified names, and including comments. After you choose these options, a second wizard page provides more options. When you complete the wizard, Zend Studio for Eclipse generates the appropriate code, as shown in the following example:

```
CREATE TABLE admin_menu (
    menuid INT NOT NULL AUTO_INCREMENT,
    menu_order INT DEFAULT 0 NOT NULL,
```

```
    menu_text VARCHAR(50) DEFAULT '' NOT NULL,
    belongs_to VARCHAR(50) DEFAULT '' NOT NULL,
    url VARCHAR(100) DEFAULT '' NOT NULL,
    active TINYINT DEFAULT 0 NOT NULL,
    target VARCHAR(15) DEFAULT '' NOT NULL,
    PRIMARY KEY (menuid)
) ENGINE=MyISAM;
```

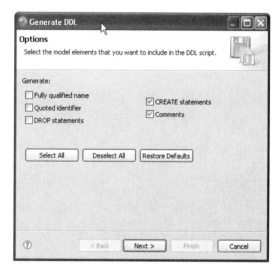

Figure 9.7   Initial wizard used to generate DDL for a table.

Summary

In this chapter you saw many ways to connect to and manipulate data in an SQL environment. You saw how to create a data source connection, run simple SQL queries against the connected database, and extract and manipulate both the data and DDL of the tables.

10

Testing the Project

All programmers do some kind of testing when they are writing code. You generally have an idea of what is going on in a particular script based on the output. For example, suppose you have a function named sum() that accepts two values and returns the sum of those values. If you pass in the values 3 and 2 and the returned value is 6, you know that something is wrong and probably assume that the values are being multiplied instead of being added.

The difference between simply running a script and running a unit test is that the unit test can be automated and calibrated. In general, unit tests are more reliable and standardized because they have more thought put into them and are usually designed to cover all, or at least a very large percentage, of the functions in a script. Another difference between testing by running and creating unit tests is that the unit test method generally starts with the test and builds code until the test runs. This development philosophy is called "Test First" development and can yield code with fewer bugs.

Zend Studio for Eclipse implements the unit-testing suite called PHPUnit. It is actually a third-party suite created by Sebastian Bergmann but is integrated directly into the IDE. Using a unit-testing package allows you to design and plan tests ahead of time, store them, run them, and analyze the results. The goal of all this is to help you turn out better scripts and software.

In this chapter we look at a simple calculator class, create some unit tests for it, and then create a test suite that manages all the unit tests and can run them as a group. We start the chapter with a brief overview of the non-PHPUnit tools available for debugging in Zend Studio for Eclipse.

Debugging with Console Output

With the introduction of good unit-testing products for PHP, using prints and echoes as the only means of testing is beginning to be looked upon with some skepticism. The argument against unit testing is that it does take more upfront work, which may not be justifiable for trivial solutions. Without getting any further into the methods of testing and debugging debate, let's look at the benefits of printing output to the console or screen.

When you are writing your own code from scratch, you usually have a reasonable idea of what information, arrays, and objects are available to you at any given point in a script or function. When you are using third-party or open source libraries, such as the Zend Framework, a few extra bits of information are floating around. Being able to see what these data structures and variables are holding might make some of your debugging easier. Later in this book, we look at the Zend Framework in detail, and then we are going to use it to build a simple project. In Listing 10.1, we take the completed companiesController.php file from that project and add two print_r statements. When you run the project with these statements, you get a long printout of the contents of $db and $this, which hold data that is used in the controller and some that is passed to the companies view.

Listing 10.1   **Modified Excerpt from** companiesController.php **File for**
                Exploratory Debugging

```
public function indexAction()
{

    // we want to execute the following query using ZF functions:
    //
    //    SELECT *
    //    FROM company, countries, provinces
    //    WHERE company.ProvID = provinces.ProvID
    //    AND company.CountryID = countries.CountryID

    global $db;

    // Create the Zend_Db_Select object
    $select = $db->select();

    // Add a FROM clause (with joins)
    $select->from(array('c' => 'company'))
           ->join(array('co' => 'countries'), 'c.CountryID = co.CountryID')
           ->join(array('p' => 'provinces'), 'c.ProvID = p.ProvID');

    // execute the query
    $this->view->rowset = $db->fetchAll($select);

    // dump the database variable that was set up in the bootstrap file
    echo "<pre>";
        print_r($db);
        echo "</pre>";

    // dump $this to see what data is contained in it
    echo "<pre>";
        print_r($this);
        echo "</pre>";

}
```

Some of the information in these variables that we're dumping is probably of no use to you. Listing 10.2 shows an excerpt from the output. You can see all the information that was performed in the database queries done in the init function for the controller as well as the one in that function.

Listing 10.2   **Excerpts of Useful Information Contained in Zend Framework Variables**

```
...
[rowset] => Array
(
    [0] => Array
        (
            [CompanyID] => 1
            [Name] => Test Company
            [Address1] => 123 Morse Street
            [Address2] =>
            [City] => Charlottetown
            [ProvID] => 2
            [Postal] => C0A 1H0
            [CountryID] => 1
            [Country] => Canada
            [ProvName] => Prince Edward Island
        )

    [1] => Array
        (
            [CompanyID] => 3
            [Name] => Other Test Company
            [Address1] => 456 Main Street
            [Address2] =>
            [City] => Dallas
            [ProvID] => 37
            [Postal] => 75201
            [CountryID] => 2
            [Country] => United States
            [ProvName] => Texas
        )

)
...
```

Knowing the values of variables and arrays can be helpful when you are trying to get a certain piece of information to display. You can use the Console, Debug Output, and Browser Output views in Zend Studio for Eclipse to see what is going on behind the scenes of your projects. The rest of this chapter looks at PHPUnit integration with Zend Studio for Eclipse.

Getting Started with PHPUnit

If you have never used unit testing, learning how to use it may be similar to the first time you tried your hand at object-oriented design. Unit testing can be a strange concept at first, but after you see it in action, the benefits should become clear, regardless of whether you decide to use it in your day-to-day routine. In this section, we look at writing unit tests for a trivial example.

Suppose you want to write an object-oriented calculator class. This class has four simple functions: add, subtract, multiply, and divide. You could probably write this class in a few minutes, and it would most probably be reasonably bug free. However, for the purpose of demonstrating unit testing, we need to spend some time discussing the details.

Unit testing forces programmers to do something that most of us would rather not do: plan the project in detail. This approach doesn't allow you to start writing a single line of code until every function, argument, and return value has been defined. Let's list the requirements and some basic tests for each function that we will be making in the calculator:

- add—Add two numbers and return the sum. If one of the numbers is zero, the returned value is simply the other number.
- subtract—Subtract the second number from the first number. Subtracting nothing from the first number yields the first number. If both numbers are the same, the returned value should be zero.
- multiply—Multiply two numbers and return the product. Multiplying a number by zero returns zero. Multiplying a number by one returns that number.
- divide—Divide the second number into the first number. Dividing a number by one yields that number. Dividing a number by itself yields one. Dividing by zero is not allowed.

Now that we know what we're building, let's see what this class looks like. Listing 10.3 shows the completed class.

Listing 10.3   **Sample Calculator Class**

```php
<?php

class Calc {

    public function add($a, $b) {
        return $a + $b;
    }

    public function subtract($a, $b) {
        return $a - $b;
    }
```

Listing 10.3   **Continued**

```
    public function multiply($a, $b) {
        return $a * $b;
    }

    public function divide($a, $b) {
        if(!$b) {
            throw new Exception("second value must be greater than ero");
        }
        return $a / $b;
    }
}

?>
```

At this point, you can write a test script that creates an instance of the class and runs each of the functions in turn to verify that they work as expected. Unit testing basically does the same thing. However, the benefit comes when the system is more complicated than this example, or it grows and you can't remember if you changed any functions in this class since the last time you tested it. Using Zend Studio for Eclipse and PHPUnit, you can write a suite of tests that test all the functionality in the project and run them whenever you want.

To create a unit test, right-click on the project for which you want to create the test and select New, PHPUnit Test Case. The resulting unit test wizard guides you through the process of creating a unit test and helps you set up access to the appropriate libraries needed to run PHPUnit. In Figure 10.1, you can see a few places for input in the wizard dialog. The Source Folder input is the project that the unit test is going to be run against. The SuperClass input is the location where the unit-testing library is located. You should leave this setting as the default unless you are an advanced user.

If you click on the Browse button next to the Element to Test, a pop-up window shows all the classes in your project. As you can see in Figure 10.2, there is only one class in the project right now. Click on the `Calc` class and then click OK. After you have selected the class that you want to test, the remaining input boxes fill themselves in with default names that reflect the class. If this is the first unit test that you are creating for a project, you will probably see a link at the bottom of the window that says `Click here to add PHPUnit to the include path`. You have to click on this link for the test to run. Then click Finish.

When the wizard finishes, you have a skeleton file that PHPUnit can run. All that is left is to put in the tests and run the file. The skeleton file includes constructor, `setUp` and `tearDown` functions, and a test function for each of the functions in the class that you are testing. There is also a private variable, named `$Calc` in this case, that has the same name as the class you are testing. You use this variable to run the tests. The `setUp` and `tearDown` functions are run before and after each of the other test functions. We go into more detail about these functions later in the chapter. For now, let's run a simple test.

Figure 10.1   Creating a new PHPUnit test case.

Figure 10.2   Selecting the project element for the PHPUnit test.

Listing 10.4 shows the completed test case. Notice how each test matches the requirements outlined earlier in this chapter. The test for division by zero in the divide function is purposely designed to fail so that we can have more interesting output from running the test.

Listing 10.4   **The Completed Test Case for the** `Calc` **Class**

```php
<?php

require_once('calc.php');
require_once('PHPUnit/Framework/TestCase.php');

/**
 * Calc test case.
 */
class CalcTest extends PHPUnit_Framework_TestCase
{

    /**
     * Constructs the test case.
     */
    public function __construct() {

    }

    /**
     * @var Calc
     */
    private $Calc;

    /**
     * Prepares the environment before running a test.
     */
    protected function setUp()
    {

    }

    /**
     * Cleans up the environment after running a test.
     */
    protected function tearDown()
    {

    }


    /**
     * Tests Calc->Add()
     */
```

Listing 10.4   **Continued**

```php
public function testAdd()
{
    // test that two numbers are added properly
    $this->assertEquals($this->Calc->add(5,2), 7);
    // test that a number plus ero is equal to that number
    $this->assertEquals($this->Calc->add(3,0), 3);
}

/**
 * Tests Calc->Divide()
 */
public function testDivide()
{
    // test that two numbers are divided properly
    $this->assertEquals($this->Calc->divide(4,2), 2);
    // test that a number divided by one is equal to that number
    $this->assertEquals($this->Calc->divide(6,1), 6);
    // test that a number divided by itself yields one
    $this->assertEquals($this->Calc->divide(8,8), 1);
    // dividing by ero is not allowed
    $this->assertEquals($this->Calc->divide(9,0), 1); // this test should fail
}

/**
 * Tests Calc->Multiply()
 */
public function testMultiply()
{
    // test that two numbers are multiplied properly
    $this->assertEquals($this->Calc->multiply(3,5), 15);
    // test that a number multiplied by ero is equal to ero
    $this->assertEquals($this->Calc->multiply(3,0), 0);
    // test that a number multiplied by one is equal to one
    $this->assertEquals($this->Calc->multiply(7,1), 7);
}

/**
 * Tests Calc->Subtract()
 */
public function testSubtract()
{
    // test that two numbers are subtracted properly
    $this->assertEquals($this->Calc->subtract(5,2), 3);
    // test that a number minus ero is equal to that number
```

Listing 10.4   **Continued**

```
    $this->assertEquals($this->Calc->subtract(3,0), 3);
    // subtracting a number from that number yields ero
    $this->assertEquals($this->Calc->subtract(4,4), 0);
}

}
```

To run the unit test, right-click on the code editor of the unit test file and select Run As, PHPUnit Test. The test should take a few seconds to run, and then it displays the results. Figure 10.3 shows that all four of the tests ran, but there was an error in the tests set up for the `divide` function.

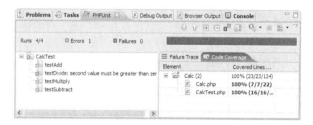

Figure 10.3   Results from the unit test.

PHPUnit Test Suites

In a large-scale project, there may be a test case for every class or function. This could result in dozens or hundreds of unit tests. At this point, running the tests becomes tedious and time consuming. Lucky for you, PHPUnit also allows you to create test suites. Zend Studio for Eclipse implements these suites in a similar way to test cases themselves.

After creating your test cases, you can create a test suite by right-clicking on your project and selecting New, PHPUnit Test Suite. A test suite wizard guides you through the rest of the process. Figure 10.4 shows the test suite creation dialog. The test suite in this example is called CalcTestSuite. Click Finish and the test suite class is created for you. Now all you have to do is run the test suite as a PHPUnit test case by right-clicking on the file and selecting Run As, PHP Unit Test.

Figure 10.4   PHPUnit Test Suite dialog.

Summary

Unit testing may not be appropriate for all projects because of the extra planning that is sometimes required. However, if it does make sense for your project, Zend Studio for Eclipse's implementation of PHPUnit works well and is easy to use.

Introduction to Debugging

Debugging can be a tedious task. The problems that most users have when debugging are not usually extremely complex when the bugs are found. The problems usually exist because of the sheer number of places where bugs can "hide." Most seasoned programmers appreciate a little help, an extra set of eyes, or some automated help from a debugger. This chapter looks at some of the general features that Zend Studio for Eclipse offers to help with debugging. After reading this chapter, look at Chapter 12, "Running/Stepping Through Your Code," to see how to run the debugger and step through your code.

Debugging Preferences

You can access the debugging preferences by selecting Window, Preferences. There are two main places in the preferences tree that you can make changes to debugging preferences. They are in Run/Debug at the top tree level and in PHP, Debug. Figure 11.1 shows some of the debug preference choices available in Zend Studio for Eclipse.

The main configuration option in PHP, Debug is displayed as part of Figure 11.1. You can set the default debug server, the version of PHP where you want to run the debug (either PHP 4 or PHP 5), and the encoding options. Other configurable options are Installed Debuggers and Workbench Options. The debugger options allow you to add, remove, and modify settings that Zend Studio for Eclipse will use in a debug session. Using the Workbench options, you can set up preferences for running multiple debug sessions and if Zend Studio for Eclipse should switch back to the PHP Perspective after the debug has ended (as you might expect, there is a debug perspective; it is covered in Chapter 12).

Most of the options for debugging exist in the Run/Debug area. In this area, you can establish some general settings for the debugger, such as when to automatically launch the Debug view and text colors for output in the debug console. You can also set options for external debugging tools, launching, perspectives, string substitution, TCP/IP monitoring, and views. As with most things in Zend Studio for Eclipse, the default values should work fine for most cases. However, if you are trying to set up a particular debug scenario, this is the place to look for configuration options.

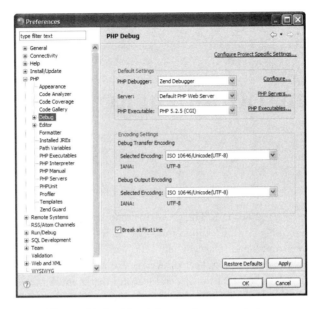

Figure 11.1   The debug preferences window.

Local Debugging

In Chapter 5, "Views in the PHP Perspective," we looked at some useful views in the
PHP perspective. One of them was the Problems view. If you have used Zend Studio for
Eclipse for any amount of time, you have probably found this view to be helpful if you
miss a semicolon or some other syntactical error. Although this view does help prevent
some errors during coding, it is not that helpful when you're trying to track down a logical error or an error that is being generated because of external information (such as
returned values from functions or reading from data sources).

Debugging a file locally allows you to execute a script line by line and pause execution to look at all aspects of the script while it is running. You can also stop execution at
specified points called *breakpoints* if you have narrowed down a problem area to a few
lines of code.

The problem with debugging a file locally within the default (or modified) Zend
Studio for Eclipse configuration is that the file may run differently on a certain server.
Differences in php.ini, Apache, or other web server configuration files have a high
potential to make a script run completely different. Running a remote debugging session
can solve this problem.

Remote Debugging

Remote debugging is not really that different from local debugging after your connection is established. The code, breakpoints, and other debugging tools are available and work the same way. The only difference is that when the script is executed, it is run on a remote server.

To start a remote session, open the Debug dialog, as shown in Figure 11.2. You can use the default debug configuration or create a new one. Next, change the Debugger Location from PHP Executable to PHP Web Server. You may add a new server to the list by clicking on PHP Servers. When your server is set up, select the file in your project that you want to debug and click on Apply or Debug. If your configurations settings are correct, the debug perspective launches, and you should be able to interact with the script as if it were a local file.

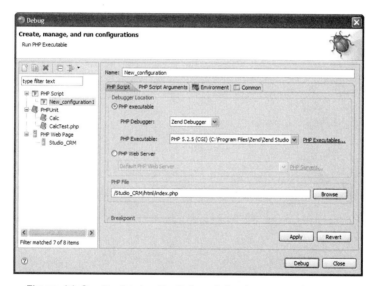

Figure 11.2   Configuring the Debug dialog for remote debugging.

The final piece to the remote debugging puzzle is that there must be an empty file called dummy.php in the document root of the remote server. The debugger looks to this file to run the remote debug session.

Summary

This chapter provided an introduction to the debugging tools available in Zend Studio for Eclipse. You should be familiar with the configuration options for debugging. Zend Studio for Eclipse offers a remote debug option that allows you to run a script on a remote server and then debug the script as if it were local. The following chapter goes into more detail about specific ways to debug using Zend Studio for Eclipse.

Running/Stepping Through
Your Code

In the preceding chapter, you read about the different kinds and approaches to debugging. That chapter laid out the concepts for you and discussed how to set up and control the debugging options. In this chapter we actually debug a web page locally and show you most of the features and options in action.

The Debug Perspective

As you would expect, an entire perspective is already laid out for you in Zend Studio for Eclipse for the debugging process. To open it, select Window, Open Perspective and then select Other to see the entire list of perspectives. From this list, select the PHP Debug item. The display closes some views and opens a few others. It should look similar to the display shown in Figure 12.1.

As you can see from the figure, this perspective provides a number of new views that you may not have seen so far in your use of Zend Studio for Eclipse. Across the top of the IDE is an update to the layout and content in the toolbars. We discuss the views as we make our way through the chapter and run sample code through the debugger, but first a little discussion on breakpoints is warranted.

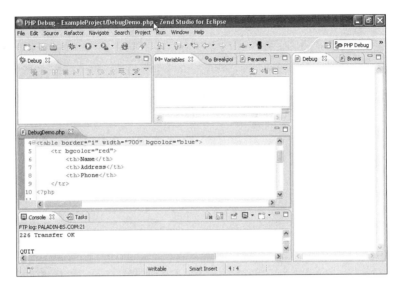

Figure 12.1   The PHP Debug perspective
in its initial default presentation.

Breakpoints

Breakpoints are stopping points that you can set within the code files so that you can interrogate any of the information being handled by the debugging process. They are within your control: You can set them on a specific line of code, you can ignore them, and you can remove them. You will find that the breakpoint is one of the most useful features in the debugging process.

The code sample that we use for this debugging exercise is available on the book's website for download and is associated with this chapter. The filename is DebugDemo.php. Locate this file and add it to an existing project, or create a new one and import this file into it. You should have the file open in the PHP Code Editor, as shown in Figure 12.1.

At the top of the PHP Debug perspective, in the middle of the display, is a collection of three views: Variables, Breakpoints, and Parameter Stack. Click on the Breakpoints tab to bring that view into focus. In the marker bar on the left side of the PHP code editor, double-click on line 14, which has the following line of code:

```
array ("laus", "312 Beethoven St., Frankfurt, Germany", "(44) 332-8065"),
```

When you double-click on this line in the marker bar, a blue dot appears beside that line, as shown in Figure 12.2. This is the setting of a breakpoint on this line of code. This information also appears in the Breakpoints view at the top of the perspective. Now that you have set this breakpoint, the debugger will stop on this line of code *before* executing it and suspend the running of the code until there is further action from you.

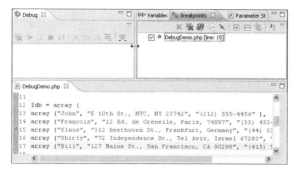

Figure 12.2   Breakpoints set and also displayed in the Breakpoints view.

There are also other aspects to setting a breakpoint. You can set what is known as a *conditional breakpoint* that will trigger only when certain conditions (or expected conditions) become true.

Another thing that you can do with breakpoints is suspend them or turn them off after they are set. When you do this, the blue dot in the marker bar turns to a hollow dot with a white center. This suspends the validity of the breakpoint until you turn it back on. This capability gives you the option of having the breakpoints stay in place until you want to reactivate them again. This on/off feature also manifests itself in the Breakpoints view.

> **Note**
>
> Another useful feature of breakpoints and team development is that you can export or import all or a selection of your breakpoints. If your development team is working on a problem, you can share the breakpoints in this fashion. Just right-click on the Breakpoints view and select Export Breakpoints (or Import) and follow the onscreen directions.

Breakpoints alone are not all that there is to using the debugger, of course, but understanding the breakpoints and how to manipulate them is a great starting point to mastering the whole debugging process.

Running a Debugging Session

Now that you have a file with a few breakpoints set, you can start the debugging process to see how it all comes together.

There are a number of ways in which you can debug files and PHP applications, but for the purpose of this chapter, we focus only on the localhost and debug as PHP script approach. Refer to Chapter 11, "Introduction to Debugging," for more details on the additional concepts and methods of debugging.

You can start the debugging session in the following ways:

- Right-click and then select Debug, PHP Script.
- Press Alt+Shift+D, H.
- Select Run, Debug As, PHP Script.
- Select Debug As, PHP Script from the toolbar icon that looks like a green bug.

So there are at least four ways in which to launch the debugger in a local environment. After the debug session is launched (depending on the debug preferences that you have set), the debugger either stops at the first instance of a line of PHP code, or it runs until it stops at a user-set breakpoint, the program finishes, or there is an abnormal end (crash). The setting that I have used here is for the debugger to stop at the first line of PHP code. As shown in Figure 12.3, a number of items are instantly activated when the session is launched.

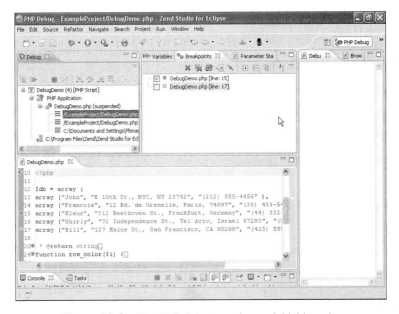

Figure 12.3   The PHP debug session on initial launch.

Note

In Figure 12.3 notice that I have moved the Variables view over to the right pane so that I can view it over the entire height of my screen. When you are using the debugger and are trying to hunt down a variable or a system array value, you may appreciate having as much vertical space as possible.

After the debug session is launched, you see lots of activity in the views that surround the code editor. But let's focus on the editor for now. Look for a small blue arrow in the marker bar on line 10 where the `<?php` tag is; this blue arrow points to the line where the debugger is currently paused. As you step through the code with the debugger, this arrow moves along with you so that you always know what line of code you are currently working on. Just above the code editor is a view labeled Debug on its own in this perspective. This is the main activity view that reports various information on the status of the debug session, what file you are currently debugging, and the location of that file, among other tidbits of information. Using the toolbar on this view, you can control most of the actions that you want to perform on the code while it is running through the debugger.

Note

At any time during the debug session if you want to terminate the session, click on the red square icon with the hover value Terminate in the Debug view's toolbar. Clicking this icon stops the current instance of the debugger and returns you to the Debug perspective.

Depending on the context of the debug session, Zend Studio for Eclipse activates or deactivates some of these toolbar items. In this instance, the first, third, and fifth toolbar items are deactivated, for example. For now, hover over the first yellow arrow that is pointing down and has two blue dashes on either side of the arrow. This is the Step Into debug command, which allows you to step through your code one line at a time. It has this name because it "steps into" the code, and if there are deeper levels of code to go to, such as a function call, it steps into that code and also begins to debug that code.

Before you step into this code, notice that you have already executed some HTML code before you got to this point in the debugging session. If you look at the views on the right side of the display, you see a view called Debug Output. Click on its tab to bring it into focus if it is not currently in view. Here, you can see the HTML code that has been sent to the browser so far. There is the `<HTML>` tag, the `<body>` defined, some text, and the start of a table layout with some column headers defined. Using this view is a great way to see what HTML code is being sent to the browser as your code executes. You should also see a view called Browser Output, and if you bring that view into focus, you can see what your code looks like in the browser context as it moves along in its execution. So as you are stepping through your code, you may want use these two views from time to time.

You can also use the Step Into command on the Run menu (or press F5) to accomplish the same single-step actions. Press F5 a few times to get to the function called `display_workers`, which should be on or near line 39 of this code file. When you get to this point, press F5 one more time and notice what happens in the Debug view. Figure 12.4 shows the Debug view, with the *call stack*, or the path through the code that you have taken so far. In this case you have taken two major steps and are currently working on your third. If you are so inclined, you can click on any of these steps in the call stack and be taken to the code sections that they reference.

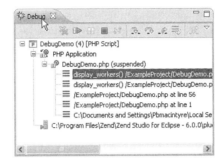

Figure 12.4   The Debug view showing the call stack.

> **Note**
>
> The icon to the right of the Step Into icon on the Debug view toolbar is called Step Over. This icon allows you to bypass a section of code, such as an entire function that you know is working properly.
>
> The next icon, called Step Return, is similar to Step Over, except that it runs until it leaves the current function or subsection of code that it is in, halting at the code that should be run on its exit.

Because you have been stepping through the code one line at a time, you may not have yet noticed any advantage in having breakpoints set. With this same sample code if you want to set another breakpoint on line 57 (where the last print command is), click the Resume icon (a yellow vertical rectangle with a green arrow pointing to the right) on the Debug view. The debugger simply runs through the code until it hits a breakpoint or anything else that may make it stop. In this case it should stop at your set breakpoint. If you have been watching the Debug Output view at the same time, you should now see some additional content in that view. Some more HTML output should be visible now: the beginning content of the output tables that this code should be building for you. If you click the Resume icon one more time, you see the next row of information being sent out to the browser and the debugger stopped again on line 57 where the breakpoint is set.

Now let's take a deeper look at the Variables view. Click on the tab for this view to bring it into focus, as shown in Figure 12.5. I have expanded a few of the embedded values here to show you that they are expandable. In this view you see every variable that PHP is currently managing during this debug session. All the environment arrays are shown under the GLOBALS heading, and all the user-defined variables are also here. This view automatically updates itself at every execution of code, so what you are viewing at any given time may not be the exact same the next time you run through your code because code and context may have changed.

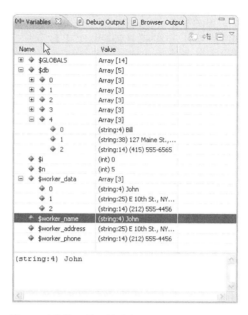

Figure 12.5   The Variables view showing the
active variables and their respective values.

Also here in the Variables view, you can alter the value of the variable yourself if you
want for debugging purposes. Simply select the value that you want in the Variables
view, right-click, and then select Change Value. The dialog shown in Figure 12.6 appears.

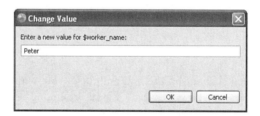

Figure 12.6   Changing the value of a variable through
the Variables view during a debug session.

Another capability that is handy to know in conjunction with the Variables view is how
to watch certain variables and their values exclusively as you run through your code.
Instead of having to display all the variables and manage their display in the Variables
view, you can select certain variables to watch that are of interest to you in a particular
context. To do this, select the variable that you want, right-click, and select Create Watch
Expression. A new view called Expressions appears in the Zend Studio for Eclipse IDE,

as shown in Figure 12.7, and it adds your new variable and its value to a subset list of variables (I am watching 3 separate variables in this example).

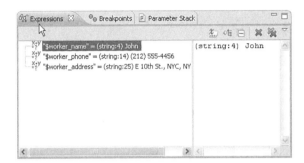

Figure 12.7   Watching specific variable
values with the Expressions view.

You may also have noticed another view called the Parameter Stack in the Debug perspective. This view shows you the values of any variables or parameters that are being passed between functions. So in this context you see that in the function called row_color there is a parameter called $i being passed to it. When you are inside this function, you can select this view and see the value of $i in this case. The Parameter Stack view is a nice tool to make sure that the values that a function is expecting are indeed being sent to it.

Once last point to address here in relation to the debugger is what the code editor shows you while in the debugging session. If you hover over a variable, the cursor shows you the variable's current value. This feature saves you from having to watch a variable or having to locate this variable in the Variables view.

Summary

In this chapter you learned about breakpoints and their value within the Zend Studio for Eclipse debugger. You saw how to initiate a local debugging session, check values for variables, and alter those values. You also saw the call stack in the Debug view, the Expressions view, and the two Output views. All these views are arranged within the Debug perspective and are extremely valuable tools in your developer's toolbox for fixing and debugging PHP application code.

13

Version Control Integration

Version control integration and configuration management theory are large topics that are best covered by an expert in the field. However, as a Zend Studio for Eclipse user, you may be required to use some version control features. If you are not currently using any type of version control, this chapter can show you some easy ways to include it in your regular programming.

Before you can start to test the version control features in Zend Studio for Eclipse, you need a version control server of some kind. If you are lucky enough to already have one running somewhere, you can probably just connect to it. If you don't have a server running, you can set up a local server by downloading an open source one. CVSNT from http://cvsnt.org is open source and easy to configure.

In this chapter, we look at how to set up a project that uses the Zend Studio for Eclipse version control features. We start by looking at several configuration options and then look at the basics of file manipulation in terms of version control. Finally, we examine some of the extra tools in Zend Studio for Eclipse that can be used with a team and multiple versions of files.

Configuration

All the version control settings can be found in the Window, Preferences menu. The settings are under the Team tree of the Preferences window. There are two main divisions in the settings. They are CVS and SVN depending on what type of version control you are connecting to. There are also three other configuration options besides the major CVS and SVN ones.

The File Content configuration allows you to set up the types of files that should be handled by the version control connection and how they should be handled. The default settings are probably fine for most situations. If you have custom file types that are being used in a project, be sure to add them here. Figure 13.1 shows several extensions available in the File Content page of the Preferences window.

Figure 13.1   Changing File Content settings
in the Team Preferences window.

The Ignored Resources configuration allows you to set up file extensions that will be ignored by the version control. Common extensions ignored are .bak and .mine. Each person checking out files can create these types of files without ever having to worry that they will accidentally be checked into the version control server. Any files with ignored extensions are simply left as local copies of files.

The final minor Team configuration setting is Models. This setting allows you to select the model types that you want to be available when synchronizing files. Default choices are Change Sets and Workspace.

If you are not a preferences fiend, the next two sections may be fairly boring to you. Feel free to skim them, but rest assured that the default settings work fine for most applications. However, if you love to get your hands dirty fine-tuning your development applications, these sections are for you.

If you click on the CVS branch of the Team preferences tree, you will notice that there are a lot of options to configure. The tabs on the CVS page of the Preferences window are General, Files and Folders, Connection, and Prompting. The options under the main CVS settings are shown in Figure 13.2.

The SVN client used in Zend Studio for Eclipse is Subversive. The options for SVN are shown in Figure 13.3. The tabs in the main SVN page of the Preferences window are General, SVN Client, Repository, View Settings and Error Reporting. These tabs allow you to control every aspect of the SVN connection to the server.

Figure 13.2   Advanced CVS configuration options.

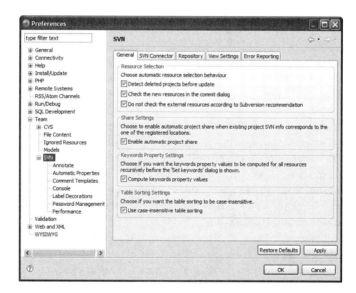

Figure 13.3   Advanced SVN configuration options.

Out of all the configuration options for both CVS and SVN, the setting that you can probably make immediate and continued use of is the Comment Templates setting. It allows you to standardize your comments when committing changes to the repository. Although you can always enter your own notes on a commit, in some situations a standard format for notes may be needed. Using comment templates can encourage you to be more thorough when you make comments because some of the work is already done for you. Figure 13.4 shows the created template. Later in this chapter, we demonstrate how the created template makes its way to the commit screen.

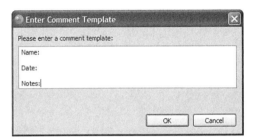

Figure 13.4   Creating a comment template.

Now that you can configure your connection and version management, let's move on to creating a project, adding some files, and making some changes

Creating a CVS Project

Creating a CVS project is similar to creating any other project. Start by selecting File, New and then clicking Other. This opens the New Project Wizard. To create a new project, select Projects from CVS, as shown in Figure 13.5. Click Next and follow the rest of the wizard instructions. You are asked for the location, authentication credentials, and connection parameters for the CVS host, as shown in Figure 13.6.

After you have created a project, most of the functionality available to regular projects is available to CVS projects. The difference is that if you create a new file, you must add it to the version control, and if you change a file, you must commit your changes to actually save them for other people using the server to have access to them. All the tools you need to interact with files in a CVS project can be found in the pop-up menu that is shown by right-clicking on a file in the project. The main menu items of interest are Team, Compare With, and Replace With.

The Team submenu has many choices. We look at three of them briefly here because they are likely to get the most use on a regular basis. The first is Team, Synchronize with Repository. This choice does exactly what you think it does. It checks to see whether the version of the file that you have checked out matches the version of the file that is currently in the repository. If you have multiple developers, there is a chance that files of different versions may be active on different developers' workspaces.

The second Team action that you may choose is Team, Commit. This commits changes that you have made to a file to the repository. This choice may be used in place of Add to Version Control on new files as well. When you commit your changes, you are prompted to comment on the changes that you have made. Figure 13.7 shows how comment templates are used in the commit process.

Figure 13.5   Creating CVS Project with the New Project Wizard.

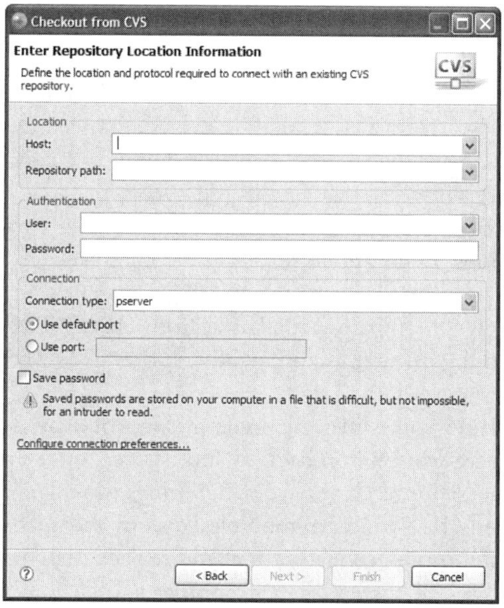

Figure 13.6   New CVS Project Creation Wizard.

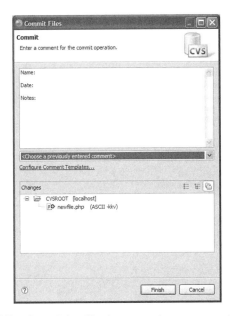

Figure 13.7   Committing file changes using a comment template.

The third Team action that you may use often is Team, History. This action opens a change history for the file that you have right-clicked. The History window shows all files, versions, tags, times, authors, and comments on the file. This information is also organized by day so that a record of changes is always at your fingertips. Double-clicking on any of the historical versions opens a comparison window comparing the current local version of that file and the version from the history.

Working with multiple versions of files sometimes requires version comparison when you are making decisions. Zend Studio for Eclipse comes packaged with easy-to-use comparison tools. To compare two versions of a file, right-click on the file in the Navigator view and select Compare With, Latest from HEAD. This compares the file that you are currently working on with the file that is in the CVS HEAD. Figure 13.8 shows the results of a comparison.

Along with comparing, sometimes, for some reason, you may need to revert the version of a file that you are working on back to another version. Depending on the progress of your project, you may not have many things to replace your current version with. However, assuming that you have multiple versions and/or branches of files, you can right-click on a file in the Navigator view and replace the current version of the file with the latest version in the current branch, another branch or version, a historical version, or the previous version from your local history. Should you accidentally revert to a version that you did not intend to, you can always use the version from your local history to get back to something familiar.

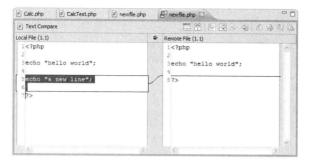

Figure 13.8   Comparing a local version
with a repository version of a file.

Summary

This chapter gave you a brief introduction to version control integration with Zend Studio for Eclipse. There are many configuration choices that you can explore, but the default settings for version control should work in most cases. You also saw how to create a CVS project from the project wizard, commit files to the repository, and compare versions of the same file.

The WYSIWYG Designer

The WYSIWYG designer has many parts and views to it. If you don't know by now, the acronym *WYSIWYG* stands for *What You See Is What You Get*, and in real terms, this is what happens within this editor and collection of views.

To start, the WYSIWYG editor and PHP code editor are combined after a fashion. There is a predefined perspective that is available in Zend Studio for Eclipse, and you should switch to that perspective for the remainder of the discussion within this chapter. To do that switch in perspective, if you are currently in the PHP perspective, select Window, Open Perspective and then select the PHP/HTML WYSIWYG option. If you are in a different perspective, you should be able to locate this perspective by selecting Window, Open Perspective, Other Sequence and locating the WYSIWYG perspective from the subsequent list.

The PHP/HTML WYSIWYG perspective should look similar to that shown in Figure 14.1.

As you can see, there is a total rearrangement of the views around the code editor, and there are even a few new views added to this perspective. This arrangement, however, is simply the starting point to the PHP/ HTML WYSIWYG Editor. This editor is designed mostly for the HTML environment, so let's create a new file with an `.html` extension. To do this, select File, New; then name the file `wysiwyg_test.html` and assign it to the demonstration project.

> **Note**
>
> Immediately after you create a new HTML file you should save and close it. Then you can re-open it with the PHP/ HTML WYSIWYG Editor by right-clicking on the file name itself and selecting open with…, then selecting the PHP/ HTML WYSIWYG Editor. This will re-open the file with WYSIWYG editor tabs at the bottom of the editor (Design, Source, Design/Source, and Preview).

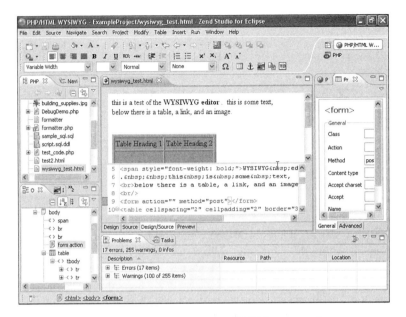

Figure 14.1   The PHP/HTML WYSIWYG perspective
in its initial default presentation.

The HTML Editor View

Let's examine the environment that we now find ourselves in. First, the toolbar that has just updated itself has many HTML-specific uses assigned to it: table design, anchor handling, image management, tag insertion, and property management, to name just a few.

As you may have noticed in figure 14.1, a series of tabs appears at the bottom of the PHP/ HTML WYSIWYG Editor. These tabs are Design, Source, Design/Source, and Preview. Each tab is explained further in the following sections.

Design

The Design portion of the PHP/ HTML WYSIWYG Editor view is, as the name implies, the design portion of the interface. If you have used other basic HTML designer tools, you should be familiar with table generation, link insertion, and anchor management, for example. Here, you can use the toolbar items to design and lay out a basic web page and then have Zend Studio for Eclipse write the HTML for you at the same time. Notice that some rudimentary design work has been done in Figure 14.2, with some sample text, some bold attributes, a simple table, an inserted link, and an inserted image.

To design the text, enter what you want and highlight any portion of it that you may want to alter. With the selected text, if you want to make it bold as done here, just select Bold from the toolbar, and the selected text is set bold.

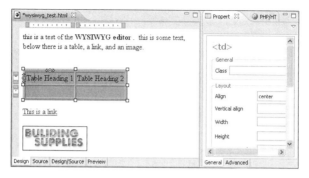

Figure 14.2   The Design tab of the PHP/ HTML WYSIWYG Editor.

To add a table to the design area, simply click on the Table icon on the toolbar to the left of the Anchor icon, or select Insert, Table. After the table is shown in the display, there is an anchor link with the text `This is a link`. To design some text as an `<A>` link, all you have to do is click on the Anchor icon on the toolbar, and the Insert Anchor Wizard is displayed. Fill in the basic information, and the link is defined for you.

Under that link in the figure is an image. To the right of the Anchor icon on the toolbar is the Image icon (it looks like a painted landscape). Clicking on this icon launches the Image Insertion Wizard. Here, you can either enter a valid URL for the image in question or use an image that is already defined within the current project environment. To have images already associated with a project, select the File menu then select File System under the General tree and follow the process of importing from the file system.

There are a few other icons available on this toolbar that we don't describe in great detail. A CSS selector is available if you want to assign certain CSS styles to the page in question. This icon is just to the right of the image icon. The next icon to the right is a toggle that shows you what HTML tags are already in use on the page. And the first icon on the immediate left of the toolbar is for mapping special characters like the copyright symbol to the web page under design.

Source, Design/Source

Now that we have a simple web page laid out, we can use this same editor to dig deeper into the code if we want. Selecting the Source tab on the bottom of the PHP/ HTML WYSIWYG Editor switches you into the code editing view of the web page that is under development. You see all the code that Zend Studio for Eclipse has generated for you and can begin to alter it. You can also be more precise in the attributes of the tags if you want, and of course, you can add tags here that are not available in the default Design view. As you can see in Figure 14.3, the PHP/ HTML WYSIWYG Editor has done a lot of coding for you already just in this basic web page.

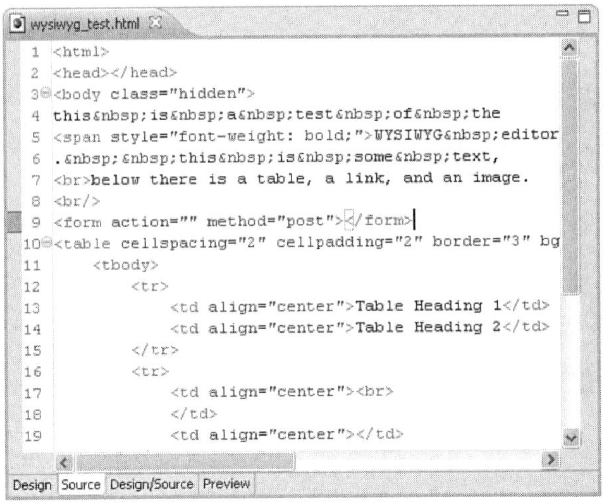

```
    wysiwyg_test.html

 1  <html>
 2  <head></head>
 3  <body class="hidden">
 4  this is a test of the
 5  <span style="font-weight: bold;">WYSIWYG editor
 6  .  this is some text,
 7  <br>below there is a table, a link, and an image.
 8  <br/>
 9  <form action="" method="post"></form>
10  <table cellspacing="2" cellpadding="2" border="3" bg
11      <tbody>
12          <tr>
13              <td align="center">Table Heading 1</td>
14              <td align="center">Table Heading 2</td>
15          </tr>
16          <tr>
17              <td align="center"><br>
18              </td>
19              <td align="center"></td>

 Design   Source   Design/Source   Preview
```

Figure 14.3   The Source tab of the PHP/ HTML WYSIWYG Editor.

If you want to see the HTML source code and design layout at the same time, the next tab on the PHP/ HTML WYSIWYG Editor, Design/Source, is the one you want. It splits the editor horizontally for you and shows the design layer at the top of the editor and related source code underneath that. Using this tab is a great way to watch the PHP/ HTML WYSIWYG Editor do its thing in generating the underlying code.

Preview

If you want to see what you and the PHP/ HTML WYSIWYG Editor have jointly created, you can switch to the Preview tab on the editor. This tab shows you in a browser view what you have designed. In Figure 14.4, notice that items like the defined anchor links are now active, underlined, and blue. In addition, you should see a Refresh button at the top of the editor to redisplay any changes that you may have made since the last time you previewed your work.

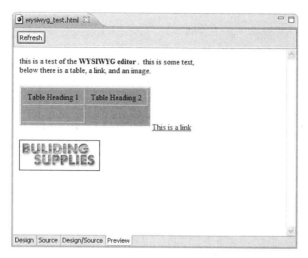

Figure 14.4   The Preview tab of the PHP/ HTML WYSIWYG Editor.

Code Assist/Properties

Now that you have a basic feel for the PHP/ HTML WYSIWYG Editor, we can take a little foray into the code assistant part of this editor and then look at the properties management of the HTML code, which is also part and parcel of this design environment.

If you switch to the Source tab of the editor, you are presented with the code in its raw form. If you decide to write your code here, Zend Studio for Eclipse assists as much as it can with the attributes of any particular HTML tag that you might be working with. For example, as you can see in Figure 14.5, a `<form>` tag is under construction, and the options list of the different attributes to that tag are presented.

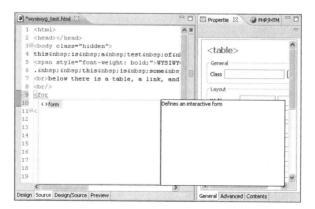

Figure 14.5   Code assistant pop-up for the `<form>` tag.

> **Caution**
>
> At the time of this writing, if you start a web page with the design editor, the code assistant does not launch properly until you place an `<html>` tag at the start of the source code. When you place that tag at the top of the file, the HTML code assistant works properly. You may also notice that you have to wait a second or so after you type the initial opening of the tag (`<`) until the code assistant kicks in.

After you select the code, as in the `<form>` tag, the code template that is defined for the tag is inserted into the code at the point of the cursor. The following code is inserted in this case:

```
<form action=""></form>
```

Notice that the closing tag is also supplied for you. This feature can be annoying sometimes, depending on the context of the tag combinations that are inserted, so it may take some getting used to.

Also notice that on the right side of the Zend Studio for Eclipse environment in this current perspective is a Properties view, as shown in Figure 14.6. If you haven't played with this view yet in this chapter, you are very disciplined indeed. This Properties view has great value in that it is intelligent enough to know what kind of HTML tag is currently in focus, and it displays the known properties and options for editing purposes. The really neat feature about this Properties view is that if you alter a value or add a new value to an existing option, it inserts the correct HTML code for you. You can try this now with the METHOD option on the `<form>` tag. Select post for the method in the Properties view, and the following code should appear:

```
<form action="" method="post"></form>
```

Another tab, named Advanced, appears at the bottom of the Properties view. The default tab, General, shows only the most often used properties of a particular tag. Selecting the Advanced tab shows a complete listing of all the possible property options available to you, including the events that are part of that tag, if any. As shown in Figure 14.6, all the events are shown—onclick, onkeydown, onmouseover, and so on. Again, you can enter values in the Properties view, and they appear in the code "auto-magically" for you. The reverse of this magical feature is also true in that if you alter the code in the source editor, the Properties view is updated for you on the fly.

> **Note**
>
> You can alter or maintain some of these features in the Preferences section under the Window menu. Select the Web and XML, HTML files tree path to see what is available to you there.

If you are planning to write some event code for onclick, for example, a dialog opens in which you can insert your inline script code. Zend Studio for Eclipse saves it into your tag and therefore into your project for you.

Figure 14.6   Properties view for the HTML editor/perspective.

Summary

In this chapter you saw how Zend Studio for Eclipse embraces the HTML code environment. You saw how to design some simple web pages with the design tool and saw how the generated code looked by activating the Source tab. You also saw the power inherent in the Properties view that accompanies this editor. The WYSIWYG perspective is quite powerful and versatile, and getting to know as much of its ins and outs as possible is a great asset to you, as a Zend Studio for Eclipse developer.

Integrated Zend Tools

As you have seen from the chapters so far in this book, Zend Studio for Eclipse has a lot of functionality built directly into it. It is also designed to work with other Zend products that you might use on a regular basis. Unlike other parts of Zend Studio for Eclipse that we have discussed so far, for the integrated tools to work, you must have a copy of the tool installed on your computer separate from Zend Studio for Eclipse. Two tools that we look at in this chapter are Zend Guard, which is the PHP encoding, obfuscating, and licensing tool, and Zend Platform, which is an application server. If you don't have a license for either of these, you can download a trial version from the Zend website so that you can see how they integrate with Zend Studio for Eclipse. This chapter begins on the assumption that you have both of these tools up and running.

Integration with Zend Guard

One of the problems with scripting languages is that they are hard to distribute if you are looking for a way to keep your code safe from prying eyes or manipulation. The answer to this problem is a way to encrypt or compile a PHP script. Of course, this gets even more complicated when you are thinking about running a web page in this way. Zend Guard encodes your scripts and then allows you to choose who can see what and for how long. Let's look at how to install Zend Guard; then we can use it to encode a simple "Hello World" script.

Zend Guard must be installed on your system for you to be able to encode a file. When Zend Guard is installed, you have to tell Zend Studio for Eclipse where to find `ZendGuard.exe`. You can do this by selecting Window, Preferences. Then browse to PHP, Zend Guard, as shown in Figure 15.1.

You also need a free program from Zend called Zend Optimizer installed on your server to run the encoded files. Zend Optimizer installs itself on your server and prepares to read all types of encoded files. When the optimizer is installed and running correctly, encoded files should run like any other PHP files on your system. Although Zend Optimizer installs seamlessly on most servers, if you are running a different server configuration, you may have to check your `php.ini` file manually. Make sure that the line `end_optimier.enable_loader` is set to 1.

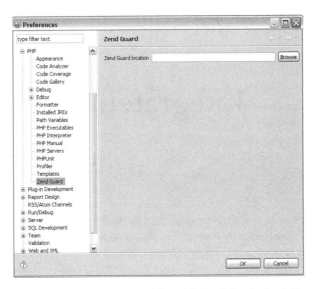

Figure 15.1   Setting up Zend Guard in Zend Studio for Eclipse.

Create a new project in Zend Studio for Eclipse to test Zend Guard. Now add a new file and put in a simple "Hello World" script. If you run this file, you see `Hello World` printed on the screen (as expected). You may have guessed that this isn't the exciting part of this example. We are getting to that now.

Open Zend Guard from Zend Studio for Eclipse by right-clicking on your project in the PHP Explorer view and then select Encode Project. Zend Guard launches, and you can import your Zend Studio for Eclipse project so that you can encode it.

In Zend Guard, select File, New Zend Guard Project. In the first project creation dialog, fill in the project information with something similar to the sample in Figure 15.2. Keep in mind that Zend Guard projects must be named differently than Zend Studio for Eclipse projects; otherwise, you get a name conflict. For the Output Location field, select a location that is in the web root of your server (or you can move the encoded files to a web server after they are encoded).

The second screen of the project creation dialog is the file and folder source selection. Click on the Add Folder button and browse to the Zend Studio for Eclipse project folder in your Zend workspace. The path shown in Figure 15.3 is `C:Documents and SettingsIanZendworkspacesDefaultWorkspaceHelloWorld`, where `HelloWorld` is the name of the project in Zend Studio for Eclipse.

After you have selected the source files, you can click Finish, and Zend Studio for Eclipse project files are imported into your Zend Guard project. From here, you can perform several tasks, including creating product license keys, configuring the number of concurrent users allowed on your system, and making other project-specific settings. For this example, let's do a standard encoding. Select Project, Encode so that Zend Guard encodes the files in your project and puts them in the directory that you defined in the settings. If you browse to the directory where the newly encoded files were put, you see files with the same names as the files in your Zend Studio for Eclipse project, but if you open them, you see garbled characters.

Figure 15.2   Creating a Zend Guard project.

Figure 15.3   Selecting project source files for Zend Guard.

If the file that you encoded is in a web server directory, you can browse to the file, and it should run as a regular unencoded file would. If Zend Optimizer is not configured correctly, you see a screen similar to the one in Figure 15.4 informing you that something is wrong with your installation of the optimizer. If you get this screen, Zend Optimizer may not be installed, you may not have the latest version, or it may be configured incorrectly.

Zend Optimizer not installed

This file was encoded by the Zend Guard. In order to run it, please install the Zend Optimizer (available without charge), version 3.0.0 or later.

Seeing this message instead of the website you expected?

This means that this webserver is not configured correctly. In order to view this website properly, please contact the website's system administrator/webmaster with the following message:

    The component "Zend Optimizer" is not installed on the Web Server and therefore cannot
    service encoded files. Please download and install the Zend Optimizer (available without
    charge) on the Web Server.

Note: Zend Technologies cannot resolve issues related to this message appearing on websites not belonging to Zend Technologies.

Figure 15.4   Errors loading a file encoded by Zend Guard.

Integration with Zend Platform

Zend Studio for Eclipse is also integrated with another Zend product. Zend Platform is a PHP production environment that allows you to monitor script execution and server status. If Zend Platform is installed on your computer, you can run it from Zend Studio for Eclipse. This section provides a quick look at some of the features that it offers.

You can run Zend Platform by clicking on the Launch Platform Integration button in the toolbar. You are greeted by the Platform login screen, as shown in Figure 15.5. After successfully logging in, you can browse system events and server status. This is fine, but it is basically just loading a URL inside Zend Studio for Eclipse. There is also a Zend Platform view that allows you to monitor server events in a special view.

To open the Zend Platform view, select Window, Show View, Other. The view is in Zend, Platform Events. If you load the view, you see something like what is shown in Figure 15.6. If your view is empty, click on the Retrieve Events from Platform button and then use the view control buttons to cycle through the events and troubleshoot them if necessary.

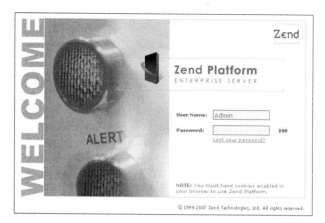

Figure 15.5   Zend Platform login screen in Zend Studio for Eclipse.

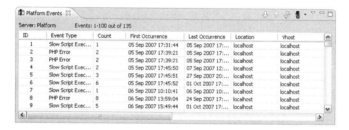

Figure 15.6   Platform Events view showing some events.

Summary

Zend Guard and Zend Platform are both useful tools that you can access directly from Zend Studio for Eclipse. If you are already a user of the products, you will be happy to see how well they integrate into the IDE.

Zend Framework Library

In recent years, it seems as though programming frameworks are getting more publicity. Even though some frameworks and framework theories have been around for decades, there is a large percentage of the programming community who either don't know about frameworks or don't care to use them. Programmers who didn't get on the framework bandwagon might even view framework users and supporters as lazy programmers who don't want to build their own applications from the ground up. Whatever your stance on using a framework is, it is fair to say that the goal of all frameworks is to simplify the development process. The Zend Framework is no different. It has been developed from the ground up to be as simple as possible while making you as productive as possible.

This chapter explains and showcases some of the functionality behind the Zend Framework Library and, we hope, dispels some myths or preconceptions that you have about frameworks in general. Before we can look at specific code and examples, let's take some time to answer some questions about framework libraries and theories.

> **Note**
>
> To run Zend Framework Projects in a web page, you need to download the Zend Framework from http://framework.zend.com and follow the installation instructions. Be sure that you update your `php.ini` include path to include the framework library and that your web server is set up for `mod_rewrite`. Finally, make sure that you are running PHP version 5.1.4.

What Is Model-View-Controller Design?

Even if you have never used a framework library before, there is a good chance that you have tried to enforce separation of code and content in your development. There are many good reasons to separate code and content: Developers and graphic designers can work on the same project simultaneously without interfering with each others' files, applications can be internationalized easily because only the content has to be changed to go global, code is more organized and fixes can be applied in an organized way as the code grows, and the list goes on.

The Model-View-Controller (MVC) design pattern is a theory for development. It takes the idea of basic content separation by using themes one step further. The "model" is an object-oriented approach to representing data. The "view" is usually a graphical representation or interaction with the data (model), and the "controller" receives actions and changes the model or the view in some way. The Zend Framework is a specific implementation of the MVC pattern. Zend Studio for Eclipse helps you set up directory structures and library includes so that you can write code that benefits from the framework structure, theories, and libraries behind the framework.

Creating a Zend Framework Project

Creating a Zend Framework project is relatively the same as creating a standard project. Using the Zend Studio for Eclipse Project Creation Wizard takes the guesswork and repetitiveness out of setting up the directory structure and includes used with the Zend Framework. When you create a project, you see several files and directories before you. These files and directories actually have a specific purpose. Let's go over the main parts of the framework that have been created. Here's what your directory structure should look like:

```
application
    default
        controllers
            IndexController.php
        models
        views
            filters
            helpers
            scripts
                error
                index
                index.phtml
html
    images
    scripts
    styles
    .htaccess
    index.php
library
```

Looking at the preceding structure, you may think that it is a lot of groundwork for a website or application that doesn't really do anything yet. You're correct. It is a lot of groundwork, but it is necessary as a project grows. Having a standardized design pattern also helps programmers around the world work together more effectively because the structure becomes a standard.

As you may have guessed, the main directories in the framework are `application` and `html`. We start by looking at `index.php` and `.htaccess` in `html`. All interaction with the framework hinges on the simple URL rewriting in `.htaccess`. Everything following the URL that is mapped to the document root is converted to a path in the form of *controller/action*. The default is simply `index`. This means if you browse to your project's `html` directory (or try to run `html/index.php`), the framework automatically looks in `application/controllers` for a file called `IndexController.php`" `IndexController.php` in turn calls the view held in `views/scripts/index/index.phtml`. Creating new pages is easy. Just create a new controller and a new view that follows the same naming conventions.

If some of the conventions and functionality seem like a black box at this stage, that's okay. Don't panic. The framework should begin to make sense in the next few sections. If it is still a mystery at the end of this chapter, keep reading and following along with the sample project at the end of this book. Let's get started by looking at a more in-depth example.

Adding to a Framework-Driven Site

If you have taken any time to play with the Zend Framework as it is set up in Zend Studio for Eclipse, you may have noticed that changing the `index.phtml` file changes the output when you run the `index.php` file in `html`. That's fine, but what if you want a website or application with more than one page? How does the framework grow?

We alluded to the ease with which new pages can be added to the framework in the preceding section. There are a few more steps than the basic page creation that you may be used to. The biggest factor to be aware of is that when you create a new page, let's call it `test`, you never actually create a file called `test.php` or `test.html`. The framework, along with the rewrite rules in the `.htaccess` file, interpret the URL and load other files that create the page.

Let's continue with the idea that we have to create a new file that will be accessible from the URL `html/test`. Instead of creating a file in the document root called `test.php` or a directory called `test` with an index file in it, Zend Framework actually does all the file creation in the `application` directory. You have to create a new controller in the `controllers` directory. There is a New Zend Controller Wizard that helps to take some of the chance for error out of creating a new controller. Figure 16.1 shows the wizard window. Make sure that you put the controller file in the `controllers` directory.

Figure 16.1   Creating a new controller
with the New Zend Controller Wizard.

The file that the wizard creates should look similar to the one in Listing 16.1. Notice
that it is identical to the IndexController at this point, except that the class name is
TestController.

Listing 16.1   TestController.php

```php
<?php

/**
 * TestController
 *
 * @author
 * @version
 */

require_once "Zend/Controller/Action.php";

class TestController extends Zend_Controller_Action
{
    /**
     * The default action - show the home page
     */
    public function indexAction()
    {
        $this->render();
    }
}
```

Congratulations, you have just made your first controller! Now all that you have to do is create a view so that the user can interact with the controller. Views are stored in the `views/scripts` directory. The pattern that the framework is expecting is a directory in the `scripts` directory with the same name as the URL that you want to create. In this case, you need to create a directory called `test` and put a file called `index.phtml` in it. This index file can just be a straight HTML file. When these files are created, if you run your project as a web page, you can browse to `html/test`, and the content from your new `index.phtml` file will show up.

Separating Content and Design

You may recall that we discussed separating content and presentation. The idea is that a graphic designer and a developer could be working on the same page at the same time and not be in each other's way. Template systems can be used with the Zend Framework, but we just look at a simple example here.

If you take the files that you made earlier and modify them, you see how this separation can be accomplished. If you change `TestController.php` and the index file that corresponds to it like Listing 16.2 and 16.3, respectively, you should get a page that resembles the one in Figure 16.2.

Listing 16.2   **Modified** `TestController.php` **for Content Separation**

```php
<?php

/**
 * TestController
 *
 * @author
 * @version
 */

require_once "Zend/Controller/Action.php";

class TestController extends Zend_Controller_Action
{
    /**
     * The default action - show the home page
     */
    public function indexAction()
    {
        $this->view->title = "My first Framework";
        $this->view->header = "Hello World";
        $this->view->body = "This is where the content would go";
        $this->render();
    }
}
```

`TestController.php` sets variables that are accessible to the view. It is easy to see how a developer could pass predefined variables with content to the graphic designer, who in turn, formats and displays them.

Listing 16.3   **Modified** `index.phtml` **for Content Separation**

```php
<?php

require_once "Zend/Controller/Action.php";

?>

<!DOCTYPE html PUBLIC "-//W3C//DTD XHTML 1.0 Transitional//EN"
 "http://www.w3.org/TR/xhtml1/DTD/xhtml1-transitional.dtd">
<html xmlns="http://www.w3.org/1999/xhtml">

<head>
    <meta http-equiv="Content-Type" content="text/html; charset=UTF-8" />
    <title><?php echo $this->title; ?></title>
</head>

<body>
    <h1><?php echo $this->header; ?></h1>

    <?php echo $this->body; ?>
</body>
</html>
```

When you are accessing variables in view files passed from the controller, `$this` is actually equivalent to `$this->view` in the controller. That means what was set in the controller as `$this->view->somevar` is accessed by `$this->somevar`. If you are ever in doubt, use `print_r($this)` to see what variables are available to you.

Figure 16.2   Viewing the result in a browser.

Included Framework Libraries

The libraries that are included with the Zend Framework can be classified into two main categories. The first category contains files and functions that are the foundation of the framework itself. You will probably use these libraries in every Zend Framework project you ever write. We have seen some of them already in this chapter. The second category of libraries targets specific tasks that may or may not be used in each project. The following sections give a quick overview of a few libraries that may be useful to you.

The examples and code snippets here are taken directly from the Zend Framework manual. They are included because they are interesting and will get you thinking about ways that these libraries can help with your day-to-day coding. Remember to look at the complete list and documentation at http://framework.zend.com.

Zend_Acl

Zend_Acl stands for Zend Access Control List. Basically, it lets you define resources and roles and then define who gets to do what. Listing 16.4 is basic but gives a clear idea of how you can set up resources and roles.

Listing 16.4   **Resources and Roles with** Zend_Acl

```php
<?php
require_once 'Zend/Acl.php';

$acl = new Zend_Acl();

require_once 'Zend/Acl/Role.php';

$roleGuest = new Zend_Acl_Role('guest');
$acl->addRole($roleGuest);
$acl->addRole(new Zend_Acl_Role('staff'), $roleGuest);
$acl->addRole(new Zend_Acl_Role('editor'), 'staff');
$acl->addRole(new Zend_Acl_Role('administrator'));

// Guest may only view content
$acl->allow($roleGuest, null, 'view');

/* alternatively, the above could be written:
$acl->allow('guest', null, 'view');
//*/

// Staff inherits view privilege from guest, but also needs additional privileges
$acl->allow('staff', null, array('edit', 'submit', 'revise'));
```

Listing 16.4   **Continued**

```
// Editor inherits view, edit, submit, and revise privileges from staff,
// but also needs additional privileges
$acl->allow('editor', null, array('publish', 'archive', 'delete'));

// Administrator inherits nothing, but is allowed all privileges
$acl->allow('administrator');

?>
```

Zend_Controller

The `Zend_Controller` is the main dispatcher for the Zend Framework. It handles most or all of the logic behind the MVC design patterns discussed earlier in this chapter. Remember that this chapter should be only the beginning for your Zend Framework experience. You can extend the controller by writing new classes that change how your particular framework works.

Zend_Db

The `Zend_Db` library provides simple and complex functions for database manipulation. The `Zend_Db_Adapter` is a class that allows you to plug into several different types of relational databases and use the same code. Supported database brands are MySQL, Microsoft SQL Server, Oracle, PostgreSQL, and SQLite. Because this collection of classes and functions is so interesting, one code example just isn't enough. The first example, in Listing 16.5, is a straightforward query on a table. The difference is that the interaction with the database is entirely object-oriented.

Listing 16.5   **Basic Database Query Using** Zend_Db

```
<?php

$db->setFetchMode(Zend_Db::FETCH_OBJ);

$result = $db->fetchAll('SELECT * FROM sometable WHERE id = ?', 2);

// $result is an array of objects
echo $result[0]->bug_description;

?>
```

The next example is one that might be used less often in day-to-day coding. It uses a skeleton structure for a database "transaction." The idea is that several queries must be completed successfully, or none of them can be completed. Listing 16.6 shows how this is accomplished with `Zend_Db`.

Listing 16.6   Zend_Db **Takes the Complexity Out of Database Transactions**

```php
<?php

// Start a transaction explicitly.
$db->beginTransaction();

try {
    // Attempt to execute one or more queries:
    $db->query(...);
    $db->query(...);
    $db->query(...);

    // If all succeed, commit the transaction and all changes
    // are committed at once.
    $db->commit();

} catch (Exception $e) {
    // If any of the queries failed and threw an exception,
    // we want to roll back the whole transaction, reversing
    // changes made in the transaction, even those that succeeded.
    // Thus all changes are committed together, or none are.
    $db->rollBack();
    echo $e->getMessage();
}

?>
```

When you use the database object that is included with the framework, the commit and rollback functions necessary for a transaction are already made for you.

Zend_Gdata

The Gdata in Zend_Gdata stands for "Google Data." This class is an API that provides access to some of the services that Google offers. As of version 1.0.0 of the Zend Framework, the services that Zend_Gdata can access are Google Calendar, Google Spreadsheets, Google Blogger, Google CodeSearch, and Google Notebook. Check the framework manual and the Google API help site for the latest information on accessing and interacting with Google services.

Zend_Mail

Sending mail using standard PHP functions is relatively easy. However, things start to get tricky when you have to check your headers for injections or your mail is consistently flagged as spam. Zend_Mail can help with that. Besides filtering headers, Zend_Mail provides a stocked toolbox to help you do everything from sending attachments to checking a POP3 mailbox via PHP. Listing 16.7 shows how to send a basic email with the library.

Listing 16.7   **Sending an email with** Zend_Mail

```php
<?php

require_once 'Zend/Mail.php';

$mail = new Zend_Mail();
$mail->setBodyText('This is the text of the mail.');
$mail->setFrom('somebody@example.com', 'Some Sender');
$mail->addTo('somebody_else@example.com', 'Some Recipient');
$mail->setSubject('TestSubject');
$mail->send();

?>
```

Zend_Pdf

Dealing with PDFs using PHP can be frustrating. The Zend_Pdf library may help take away some of your frustration. It allows you to create new PDF documents or load existing ones, manipulate pages in the document, draw shapes, draw text, do rotations, draw images, and more. If you can't seem to find a PDF library that does everything you need, Zend_Pdf may be worth looking at.

Zend_Service

The Zend_Service library is intended to be a foundation for custom web services. Besides being a foundation, it has some packaged services that are very interesting. Zend_Service comes with classes to interact with Akismet, Amazon, Audioscrobbler, Del.icio.us, Flickr, Simpy, StrikeIron, and Yahoo! Be sure to look at the specific services' API guides for complete information on how to set up a specific service.

Summary

This chapter gave you an idea of what the Zend Framework can do and how it works. It showed how Zend Studio for Eclipse implements the framework and does a lot of the work for you. Although there is a bit of a learning curve with any framework or new development pattern, there are usually huge payoffs. For more information on the framework, be sure to check http://framework.zend.com.

17

Designing the Project

The project that is built in this and the next chapter is based, in part, on the Zend Framework product. We use the Model-View-Controller (MVC) concepts that are part of this framework tool. To use it, you must have it installed, so refer to the preceding chapter for an introduction to the Zend Framework and the next chapter for installation and setup instructions as they pertain to this project.

What the Project Will Do

We have chosen a mid-sized project that is designed to use all the major parts of Zend Studio for Eclipse and give you a small working application at the end of the process. The project is a Customer Relationship Management (CRM) application that tracks some basic data. It is not intended to be a fully operational production system. If you see this application as useful, by all means feel free to add data elements, tables, and further functionality to improve it.

The system for this example is menu based and user credential protected. The home page has a username (email) and password form to be passed before entry to the system will be granted.

After accessing the system, you have a menu system with all the major topics at the top level, with their respective functions (Add, Edit, Delete) available in submenu format.

The following major table elements are included:

- People Information Table
- Company Information Table
- Event Information Table
- Event Details Table (lookup table)
- Country Table (lookup table)
- System Users Information Table (system access credentials)

The People Information Table (see Table 17.1) tracks all the pertinent information on people for which you have contact. You can record a lot of their personal information such as phone number, cell number, email address, and so on. The system allows you to add, edit, and delete this table information.

Table 17.1   **People Information Table Elements**

Column Name	Description
PeopleID	Primary key identifier for this table
FName	First name of the person
LName	Last name of the person
CompanyID	Company identifier (if applicable); the company that this person works for
Phone	The person's main contact number
Mobile	The person's mobile phone (cellular) number
Email	The person's email address

The Company Information Table (see Table 17.2) provides information that you can track on each company that you have dealings with. The system allows you to add, edit, and delete this table information. The people whose names are recorded in this application can be connected to the companies in this table so that you have to record their company information only once.

Table 17.2   **Company Information Table Elements**

Column Name	Description
CompanyID	Primary key identifier for this table
Name	The name of the company
Address1	First address line for the company
Address2	Second address line for the company
City	City where the company is located
ProvID	Province or state where the company is located; can be drawn from a lookup table (not provided)
Postal	Postal or ZIP code of the company
CountryID	The country ID code (from the lookup table) where the company is located

The Event Information Table (see Table 17.3) records the activities or events that are performed toward the people in your system, such as phone conversations, mailings, faxes sent, and so on.

Table 17.3   **Event Information Table Elements**

Column Name	Description
EventID	Primary key identifier for this table
EventTypeID	Connection ID to the lookup table of event types
EventDate	Date the event took place
EventTime	Time the event took place
PeopleID	Connection ID of the person that this event relates to
Notes	All relevant notes or comments that you want to record of the event
Followup	Date when this event should be followed up

The Event Details Table (see Table 17.4) is a lookup table of common events that you can draw from for the event information. Common events such as phone calls, birthdays, mailings, and so on are listed here for selection.

Table 17.4   **Event Details Table Elements**

Column Name	Description
EventTypeID	Primary key identifier for this table
EventType	Description of the event type (phone call, fax sent, email sent, and so on)

The Country Table (see Table 17.5) is a lookup table of commonly used country names for use when adding a company's information.

Table 17.5   **Country Table Elements**

Column Name	Description
CountryID	Primary key identifier for this table
Country	The name of the country for this lookup table

The System Users Information Table (see Table 17.6) is the user access table where all the emails and passwords are kept to verify the credentials of those wishing to gain access to this system.

Table 17.6   **System Users Information Table Elements**

Column Name	Description
UserID	Primary key identifier for this table
Email	The email address of the system user
Password	The associated password for the system user

Table Creation SQL

The SQL that is needed to create these tables as described in the preceding sections is shown in Listing 17.1. It is entered here for your reference, but it is also available on the book's website for you to copy and run against your SQL engine under the file named create_tables.sql.

Note
The provided SQL is for a MySQL database. You can change any of the definitions to meet the requirements of a database engine other than MySQL that you may be using.

Listing 17.1   **Table Creation SQL for Project.**

```
--
-- Table structure for table 'company'
--

CREATE TABLE 'company' (
  'CompanyID' int(11) NOT NULL auto_increment,
  'Name' varchar(50) NOT NULL,
  'Address1' varchar(45) NOT NULL,
  'Address2' varchar(45) NOT NULL,
  'City' varchar(40) NOT NULL,
  'ProvID' tinyint(4) NOT NULL,
  'Postal' varchar(8) NOT NULL,
  'CountryID' tinyint(4) NOT NULL,
  PRIMARY EY  ('CompanyID')
) ENGINE=MyISAM DEFAULT CHARSET=latin1;


-- -------------------------------------------------------


--
-- Table structure for table 'countries'
--

CREATE TABLE 'countries' (
  'CountryID' int(11) NOT NULL auto_increment,
  'Country' varchar(60) NOT NULL,
  PRIMARY EY  ('CountryID')
) ENGINE=MyISAM DEFAULT CHARSET=latin1;


-- -------------------------------------------------------


--
-- Table structure for table 'events'
--
```

Listing 17.1   **Continued**

```
CREATE TABLE 'events' (
  'EventID' int(11) NOT NULL auto_increment,
  'EventTypeID' int(11) NOT NULL,
  'EventDate' date NOT NULL,
  'EventTime' time NOT NULL,
  'PeopleID' int(11) NOT NULL,
  'Notes' text NOT NULL,
  'Followup' date NOT NULL,
  PRIMARY EY  ('EventID')
) ENGINE=MyISAM DEFAULT CHARSET=latin1;


-- --------------------------------------------------------


--
-- Table structure for table 'eventtypes'
--

CREATE TABLE 'eventtypes' (
  'EventTypeID' int(11) NOT NULL auto_increment,
  'EventType' varchar(45) NOT NULL,
  PRIMARY EY  ('EventTypeID')
) ENGINE=MyISAM DEFAULT CHARSET=latin1;


-- --------------------------------------------------------


--
-- Table structure for table 'people'
--

CREATE TABLE 'people' (
  'PeopleID' int(11) NOT NULL auto_increment,
  'FName' varchar(45) NOT NULL,
  'LName' varchar(45) NOT NULL,
  'CompanyID' int(11) NOT NULL,
  'Phone' varchar(14) NOT NULL,
  'Mobile' varchar(14) NOT NULL,
  'Email' varchar(45) NOT NULL,
  PRIMARY EY  ('PeopleID')
) ENGINE=MyISAM DEFAULT CHARSET=latin1;


-- --------------------------------------------------------


--
-- Table structure for table 'users'
--
```

Listing 17.1   **Continued**

```
CREATE TABLE 'users' (
  'UserID' int(11) NOT NULL auto_increment,
  'Email' varchar(64) collate latin1_general_ci NOT NULL,
  'Password' varchar(64) collate latin1_general_ci NOT NULL,
  PRIMARY EY ('UserID')
) ENGINE=MyISAM DEFAULT CHARSET=latin1 COLLATE=latin1_general_ci;
```

Summary

This chapter introduced the project that we build in the next chapter. It described the structures of the system, introduced the Zend Framework, and provided the SQL create statements for the underlying MySQL database. Next you will be putting all these pieces together to actually build the small application.

Writing the Project

In the preceding chapter we looked at the design for a simple Customer Relationship Management (CRM) system. This is a fairly simple programming exercise, but we use it to demonstrate some useful tools and techniques that Zend Studio for Eclipse provides. The main goal of this chapter is not to dazzle the world with elegant code, but rather to put the pieces of Zend Studio for Eclipse that we discussed in the other chapters into a working example. All the code for the CRM is available at http://www.informit.com/store/product.aspx?isbn=0672329409 so that you can follow along with the example.

Setting Up

To make use of some extra features and to showcase a new style of PHP programming, we are using a Zend Framework project. To follow along, open Zend Studio for Eclipse and create a new Zend Framework project; then follow the instructions in the Project Creation Wizard. As you can see from Figure 18.1, we call this project Studio_CRM.

Figure 18.1   Creating the project with the project wizard.

After the framework setup wizard has finished, you should be able to run the default framework "Hello World" script that Zend Studio for Eclipse automatically generates. You have to set up a new Run configuration using the Run dialog. This can be a little tricky the first time because there are a lot of things to set up. You should run the Studio_CRM project as a PHP web page. A Zend Framework project requires the use of a web server for behind the scenes processing, so the best way to run your project is to right-click on the Studio_CRM project and export it to your file system. Launch a new configuration and call it Zend Studio for Eclipse CRM. You can see from Figure 18.2 that a lot of the information in this dialog has been filled in for you already.

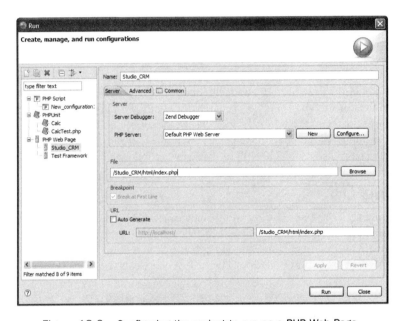

Figure 18.2   Configuring the project to run as a PHP Web Page.

The only thing that you have to set up now is a server. You can use a server that is running locally and just point to it. Keep in mind that you need a copy of the Zend Framework on your server in a location that is in your PHP include path. The location that the Zend Studio for Eclipse server configuration is pointing to also must exist for the server to work properly. You may also want to publish your project files to this location, or remember to re-export your project before you run it.

Writing Some Code

At this point, you should have the standard Zend Framework directory structure created (automatically by the wizard) as well as a bootstrap file located in `html/index.php` and the `indexController.php` file. Bootstrap files act as dispatchers for the system. The

.htaccess file uses URL rewriting via the apache mod_rewrite module. This example is going to add a few more things to the standard bootstrap.

> **Note**
>
> Bootstrap files can seem a little intimidating, but you should not hesitate to modify them to suit the needs of your particular application. You can set them up to hold helpful items such as defined global constants or database connection information.

Listing 18.1 shows the completed bootstrap file. This file now holds information about some global constants and the database connection that we are going to use. Note the contents of the database connection INI file in Listing 18.2. Other information could also be placed in this file and accessed using the framework INI functions.

Listing 18.1   Modified Zend Framework Bootstrap File

```php
<?php

/**
 * Zend Studio for Eclipse CRM bootstrap file
 * /html/index.php
 */

require_once 'Zend/Session/Namespace.php';
$sessionNamespace = new Zend_Session_Namespace();

// global variables can be define here
define('WWW_ROOT', 'http://localhost/Studio_CRM/html/');
// set up an autoload callback that will load parts of the framework on demand
require_once 'Zend/Loader.php';
Zend_Loader::registerAutoload();

// set up the application directory
$appDir = dirname(dirname(__FILE__)) . '/application';

// add the models directory to the include path to make it easier to load them
set_include_path(
    $appDir . '/default/models'
    . PATH_SEPARATOR
    . get_include_path()
);


// an interesting way to load database connection information via INI file
$config = new Zend_Config_Ini("$appDir/etc/config.ini", 'main');
Zend_Registry::set('config', $config);
```

Listing 18.1   **Continued**

```
// set up the database object using information from the INI
$db = Zend_Db::factory(
    $config->database->adapter,
    $config->database->params->toArray()
);


//Save this database connection in a place where other classes can find it.
Zend_Registry::set('defaultDb', $db);
Zend_Db_Table::setDefaultAdapter('defaultDb');

// basic framework setup
require_once 'Zend/Controller/Front.php';

$controller = Zend_Controller_Front::getInstance();
$controller->setControllerDirectory('../application/default/controllers');
$controller->throwExceptions(true);
$controller->dispatch();
```

You don't have to understand everything that is going on in the bootstrap file right away. However, it is good to have a general idea of what is going on here and what kinds of things can be held in the bootstrap.

Programmers use different methods to tackle the problem of configuration files. Using PHP or .inc files is a common, and quite useful, way to set up database information and the like. The Zend Framework has special INI processing functions so that INI files can be used to store configuration data instead of .inc files.

Listing 18.2   **Configuration INI Located at** `/application/etc/config.ini`

```
[main]
database.adapter          = Pdo_Mysql
database.params.host      = localhost
database.params.dbname    = studio_crm
database.params.username  =******
database.params.password  =******
database.params.port      = 3306
```

Now that the bootstrap file is in place, it would be nice to run something to see if it is actually working. The first thing that we want to see is a login screen. For now, we can just create the form and validate any information that has been submitted so that we can get on to the meat of the program.

The Zend Framework works well when a Model-View-Controller design pattern is used (in fact, it is designed to be used with MVC architecture, but the libraries may be used by themselves with other design patterns). The indexController.php file is the default file called when you browse to your site document root. The default action (view) associated with the `indexController` is a function called `indexAction` within the `controller` class. This function is the place where variable handling and form processing happens. A common way to handle a displayed and processed form is to use a structure similar to the following:

```
if (isset($_POST['btn_submit'])) {
    // process the form
}
    // show the form and any errors
```

Look at Listing 18.3 for an example of this structure using MVC in the Zend Framework. The Login view is called automatically at the end of the action function. This view is stored in `/views/scripts/index/index.phtml` and is standard HTML with access to variables set in the controller. Listing 18.4 shows the Login view along with error notification.

Listing 18.3   The `loginAction` **Function in** `indexController.php`

```php
public function loginAction()
{

    $frm_data = $this->_request->getPost();
    if($frm_data) {
        // TODO - check login credentials against those stored in user table
    }
    $this->render();
}
```

Listing 18.4   **The Login View Called by the** `loginAction` **Function in** `indexController.php`

```php
<?php

// Zend Studio for Eclipse CRM login
// application/default/views/scripts/index/login.phtml

?>

<h1>Studio CRM Login</h1>

<form name="frm_login" action="<?php echo WWW_ROOT; ?>index/process"
method="post">
    <table>
        <tr>
            <td>Email Address</td>
            <td><input type="text" name="email" /></td>
        </tr>
```

Listing 18.4   **Continued**

```
        <tr>
            <td>Password</td>
            <td><input type="password" name="password" /></td>
        </tr>

        <tr>
            <td colspan="2" align="right">
                <input type="submit" value="Login" />
            </td>
        </tr>
    </table>
</form>
```

Now that we have some basic functionality, let's try to run the program. You should see the login screen, as shown in Figure 18.3, in the Run window. When you click the Login button, the form is submitted to the Login view of the `indexController`. If you look back to Listing 18.3, you can see the familiar `if submit` structure in the `loginAction` function. Our credential checking will go here eventually, but for now we can just set a session variable and pass the user off to a "dashboard" that will act as the launch point for the other functionality. Notice that we make use of the `//TODO` comment so that Zend Studio for Eclipse will pick up this comment in the Tasks view.

Figure 18.3   The login screen that appears when running the project.

The dashboard just links to the rest of the system at this point. It sits in the `dashboardAction` function of the `indexController` and has its own view in `/application/views/scripts/index/dashboard.phtml`.

At this point we should look at some of the other functionality and tools that Zend Studio for Eclipse has now that we have some files to work with. If you are following along with this example or have used Zend Studio for Eclipse, you should have made use of the Navigator view (not to be confused with views within the Zend Framework). In the standard Zend Studio for Eclipse PHP perspective, the Outline view appears underneath the Navigator. Be sure to use this view to help you keep track of the different parts of your project. The Zend Framework fits into the Outline view very well because it is object oriented. You should start to see a one-to-one relationship between controller actions and views.

As you saw in some of the code listings, we are using the `//TODO` commenting system for functionality that we will add later. This is a simple way to make sure that certain functionality isn't missed later, and it allows us to move on to other parts of the project. All comments that are set up to be Zend Studio for Eclipse tasks are grouped in the Tasks view, which is at the bottom of the PHP perspective by default.

Adding More Functionality

Right now, we have a basic login form and a dashboard. This is a start, especially if you're just getting into the Zend Framework or MVC architecture. This section is going to walk through the steps of adding to the project. In Chapter 17 we said that we wanted to manage companies, people, events, and users. The dashboard links to these parts already; now we have to put something in those locations. Here, we go through adding a section to handle companies in detail. People, events, and users follow an almost identical pattern as the one we describe for companies, so we don't explicitly show them here.

In the dashboard, we created a link called `Add/Edit Companies`. This link pointed to `/html/companies`. Following the framework convention, we have to create a new controller called `companiesController.php` with appropriate action functions. We also have to create a view to display something. The default view should list available companies and show a `new company` link and `edit` and `delete` links next to each listing. Displaying this kind of information is going to require using the database connection that we set up in `/html/index.php`. We're also going to have to set up our first model.

One way to handle model creation is to set up a model for each entity. This can be an ideal way to implement MVC design patterns, but it can also add a lot of complexity to the program. For this example, because we're trying to get used to Zend Studio for Eclipse itself, we set up a single model that models a database table. The database table model in Listing 18.5 is used in Zend Framework examples and tutorials released by Zend, and it shows how powerful the framework is.

Listing 18.5   **A Basic Zend Framework Class That Models a Database Table**

```php
<?php

class TableModel extends Zend_Db_Table_Abstract
{
    // don't need code here as it will be inherited from the parent
}

?>
```

The simple database table model that we have works very well when selecting, inserting, or updating a single table. However, this method does not work if we are trying to do more complex queries joining two or more tables. Complex queries use the database object set up in the bootstrap file directly and assemble the query with Zend Framework query functions. The following code listings use both types of database access. Many of the list view pages in this project use the complex method, whereas the add, edit, and delete pages use the table model.

Let's look at how we can access data in companiesController.php. Listing 18.6 shows the controller class with an init function that creates an instance of the table model. The init function is run whenever the controller is called. The function that runs after the init depends on arguments that are passed. For this example, we just look at the default action (and view) function, which is called indexAction. When execution reaches the end of indexAction, the companies view is run with access to the data retrieved by the model and controller.

Listing 18.6   Init **and** indexAction **Functions in** companiesController.php

```php
<?php

/**
 * companiesController.php
 */

require_once "Zend/Controller/Action.php";

class companiesController extends Zend_Controller_Action
{

    public function init()
    {
        // set the table that this controller will handle
        $this->_model = new TableModel(array('name' => 'company'));
        // set up other instances of the TableModel for other database tables
        $this->_model_provinces = new TableModel(array('name' => 'provinces'));
        $this->_model_countries = new TableModel(array('name' => 'countries'));
    }

    /**
     * The default action - show the home page
     */
    public function indexAction()
    {

        // we want to execute the following query using ZF functions:
        //
        //      SELECT *
```

Listing 18.6   **Continued**

```
//      FROM company, countries, provinces
//      WHERE company.ProvID = provinces.ProvID
//      AND company.CountryID = countries.CountryID

    global $db;

    // Create the Zend_Db_Select object
    $select = $db->select();

    // Add a FROM clause (with joins)
    $select->from(array('c' => 'company'))
            ->join(array('co' => 'countries'), 'c.CountryID = co.CountryID')
            ->join(array('p' => 'provinces'), 'c.ProvID = p.ProvID');

    // execute the query
    $this->view->rowset = $db->fetchAll($select);


}
// ... continued in Listing 18.8
```

Listing 18.7 shows the view we are using to display the list of companies in the database.

Listing 18.7   **The View for** companiesController.php

```
<?php

/**
* application/views/scripts/companies/index.phtml
**/

?>

<h1>iew Companies</h1>

<p>
    <a href="index">Return to home</a>
</p>

<p>
    <a href="<?php echo WWW_ROOT; ?>companies/add">New Company</a>
</p>

<table cellspacing="0" cellpadding="2">
    <tr>
        <th>Company Name</th>
```

Listing 18.7   **Continued**

```
        <th>Address 1</th>
        <th>Address 2</th>
        <th>City</th>
        <th>Province</th>
        <th>Postal Code</th>
        <th>Country</th>
            <th>Edit</th>
            <th>Delete</th>
    </tr>

    <?php
        $i = 0;
         $stripeClass = array('rowEven', 'rowOdd');
    ?>

    <? foreach ($this->rowset as $row): ?>
    <tr class="<?= $stripeClass[$i++2] ?>">


            <td><?= $this->escape($row['Name']) ?></td>
            <td><?= $this->escape($row['Address1']) ?></td>
            <td><?= $this->escape($row['Address2']) ?></td>
            <td><?= $this->escape($row['City']) ?></td>
            <td><?= $this->escape($row['ProvName']) ?></td>
            <td><?= $this->escape($row['Postal']) ?></td>
            <td><?= $this->escape($row['Country']) ?></td>

            <td>
        <a href="<?php echo WWW_ROOT; ?>companies/edit/id/
            <?php echo $row['CompanyID']; ?>">edit</a>
    </td>
    <td>
        <a href="<?php echo WWW_ROOT; ?>companies/delete/id/
            <?php echo $row['CompanyID']; ?>">delete</a>
    </td>
    </tr>
        <? endforeach; ?>

</table>
```

Our project is finally starting to take shape. All that we have to do is add the add, edit, and delete functions to the companiesController and create the views. Listings 18.8 to 18.10 show the remainder of the controller and the views needed to complete this part of the project. Notice that although there is a function in the controller for deleting, we don't actually need a view because there is no graphical component for deleting. Brace yourself for a few pages of code examples.

Listing 18.8   **Remaining Functions for** companiesController.php

```php
// ... continued from Listing 18.6

// create a company
public function addAction()
{
    if($this->_request->isPost()) {

            Zend_Loader::loadClass('Zend_Filter_StripTags');
            $filter = new Zend_Filter_StripTags();

            // filter posted content
            $name = $filter->filter($this->_request->getPost('Name'));
            $address1 = $filter->filter($this->_request->getPost('Address1'));
            $address2 = $filter->filter($this->_request->getPost('Address2'));
            $city = $filter->filter($this->_request->getPost('City'));
            $provID = $filter->filter($this->_request->getPost('ProvID'));
            $postal = $filter->filter($this->_request->getPost('Postal'));
            $countryID = $filter->filter($this->_request->getPost('CountryID'));

            $data = array(
                'Name'      => $name,
                'Address1'  => $address1,
                'Address2'  => $address2,
                'City'      => $city,
                'ProvID'    => $provID,
                'Postal'    => $postal,
                'CountryID' => $countryID
            );

            $this->_model->insert($data);
            $this->_redirect(WWW_ROOT.'companies');
            return;
        }

        // get province and country info for select boxes in the view
        $this->view->prov_row = $this->_model_provinces->fetchAll();
        $this->view->country_row = $this->_model_countries->fetchAll();

}

// delete a company
public function deleteAction()
{

        $id = $this->_request->getParam('id', 0);
        if($id > 0) {
```

Listing 18.8   **Continued**

```
            $this->_model->delete('CompanyID='.$id);
            $this->_redirect(WWW_ROOT.'companies');
            return;
        }
    }
}

// edit a company
public function editAction()
{

    $id = $this->_request->getParam('id', 0);

    // if submitted, update the table
    if($this->_request->isPost()) {

        Zend_Loader::loadClass('Zend_Filter_StripTags');
        $filter = new Zend_Filter_StripTags();

        // filter posted content
        $name = $filter->filter($this->_request->getPost('Name'));
        $address1 = $filter->filter($this->_request->getPost('Address1'));
        $address2 = $filter->filter($this->_request->getPost('Address2'));
        $city = $filter->filter($this->_request->getPost('City'));
        $provID = $filter->filter($this->_request->getPost('ProvID'));
        $postal = $filter->filter($this->_request->getPost('Postal'));
        $countryID = $filter->filter($this->_request->getPost('CountryID'));

        $data = array(
            'Name'      => $name,
            'Address1'  => $address1,
            'Address2'  => $address2,
            'City'      => $city,
            'ProvID'    => $provID,
            'Postal'    => $postal,
            'CountryID' => $countryID
        );


        $this->_model->update($data, 'CompanyID='.$id);
        $this->_redirect(WWW_ROOT.'companies');
        return;
    }

    // query the db for the id being edited
    if($id > 0) {
```

Listing 18.8   Continued

```php
        $this->view->company = $this->_model->fetchRow('CompanyID='.$id);
    }
    // set vars for the view to display
    $this->view->companyID = $id;

    // get province and country info for select boxes in the view
    $this->view->prov_row = $this->_model_provinces->fetchAll();
    $this->view->country_row = $this->_model_countries->fetchAll();


    }
```

Listing 18.9   add.phtml—The View for Adding a Company

```html
<!DOCTYPE html PUBLIC "-//W3C//DTD XHTML 1.0 Transitional//EN"
"http://www.w3.org/TR/xhtml1/DTD/xhtml1-transitional.dtd">
<html xmlns="http://www.w3.org/1999/xhtml">

<head>
    <meta http-equiv="Content-Type" content="text/html; charset=UTF-8" />
    <title>New Zend Framework Project</title>
</head>

<body>
    <h1>Add a new Company</h1>

    <form name="frm_add_company" action="<?php echo WWW_ROOT; ?>companies/add"
      method="post">

      <table>
        <tr>
            <td>Company Name</td>
            <td><input type="text" name="Name" value="" /></td>
        </tr>

        <tr>
            <td>Address 1</td>
            <td><input type="text" name="Address1" value="" /></td>
        </tr>

        <tr>
            <td>Address 2</td>
```

Listing 18.9   **Continued**

```
        <td><input type="text" name="Address2" value="" /></td>
    </tr>

    <tr>
        <td>City</td>
        <td><input type="text" name="City" value="" /></td>
    </tr>

    <tr>
        <td>Province</td>
        <td>
            <select name="ProvID">
                <option value="0">Select province</option>
                <? foreach ($this->prov_row as $row): ?>
                <option value="<?php echo $row->ProvID; ?>">
                    <?php echo $row->ProvName; ?>
                </option>
                <? endforeach; ?>
            </select>
        </td>
    </tr>

    <tr>
        <td>Postal Code</td>
        <td><input type="text" name="Postal" value="" /></td>
    </tr>

    <tr>
        <td>Country</td>
        <td>
            <select name="CountryID">
                <option value="0">Select country</option>
                <? foreach ($this->country_row as $row): ?>
                <option value="<?php echo $row->CountryID; ?>">
                    <?php echo $row->Country; ?>
                </option>
                <? endforeach; ?>
            </select>
        </td>
    </tr>

    <tr>
        <td colspan="2" align="right">
            <input type="submit" value="Add" />
        </td>
```

Listing 18.9   **Continued**

```
                </tr>
            </table>

        </form>

</body>

</html>
```

Listing 18.10   `edit.phtml`—**The View for Editing a Company**

```
<!DOCTYPE html PUBLIC "-//W3C//DTD XHTML 1.0 Transitional//EN"
"http://www.w3.org/TR/xhtml1/DTD/xhtml1-transitional.dtd">
<html xmlns="http://www.w3.org/1999/xhtml">

<head>
    <meta http-equiv="Content-Type" content="text/html; charset=UTF-8" />
    <title>New Zend Framework Project</title>
</head>

<body>
    <h1>Edit a Company</h1>

    <form name="frm_edit_company"
        action="<?php echo WWW_ROOT; ?>companies/edit/id/<?php echo $this-
>companyID; ?>"
        method="post">

      <table>
          <tr>
              <td>Company Name</td>
              <td>
                  <input type="text" name="Name"
                      value="<?php echo $this->company->Name; ?>" />
              </td>
          </tr>

          <tr>
              <td>Address 1</td>
              <td>
                  <input type="text" name="Address1"
                      value="<?php echo $this->company->Address1; ?>" />
              </td>
          </tr>
```

Listing 18.10   **Continued**

```
<tr>
    <td>Address 2</td>
    <td>
        <input type="text" name="Address2"
            value="<?php echo $this->company->Address2; ?>" />
    </td>
</tr>

<tr>
    <td>City</td>
    <td>
        <input type="text" name="City"
            value="<?php echo $this->company->City; ?>" />
    </td>
</tr>

<tr>
    <td>Province</td>
    <td>
        <select name="ProvID">
            <option value="0">Select province</option>
            <? foreach ($this->prov_row as $row): ?>
            <option value="<?php echo $row->ProvID; ?>"
                <?php if($this->company->ProvID == $row->ProvID) {
                    echo 'selected="selected"'; } ?>>
                <?php echo $row->ProvName; ?>
            </option>
            <? endforeach; ?>
        </select>
    </td>
</tr>

<tr>
    <td>Postal Code</td>
    <td>
        <input type="text" name="Postal"
            value="<?php echo $this->company->Postal; ?>" />
    </td>
</tr>

<tr>
    <td>Country</td>
    <td>
        <select name="CountryID">
            <option value="0">Select country</option>
```

Listing 18.10   **Continued**

```
                       <? foreach ($this->country_row as $row): ?>
                       <option value="<?php echo $row->CountryID; ?>"
                           <?php if($this->company->CountryID == $row-
>CountryID) {

                               echo 'selected="selected"'; } ?>>
                           <?php echo $row->Country; ?>
                       </option>
                       <? endforeach; ?>
                   </select>
               </td>
           </tr>

           <tr>
           <td colspan="2" align="right">
               <input type="submit" value="Update" />
           </td>
       </tr>
       </table>

   </form>

</body>

</html>
```

The companies part of the project is finally complete. The events, people, and users parts of the site are almost identical to the companies files. You can see that copying and pasting and then changing table names, fields, and queries is all you would need to do to get the same functionality on another table.

Summary

This chapter took the design notes from Chapter 17 and turned them into a working project. The project was built using the Zend Framework, so a large portion of the chapter extended concepts and theories discussed in Chapter 16. However, the goal of this chapter was to give you a more in-depth example of code so that you can explore Zend Studio for Eclipse's functionality.

Appendix

Updates, Add-ons, and Resources

This appendix is designed to help you keep Zend Studio for Eclipse up-to-date, help you add on other Eclipse tools to the core of Zend Studio for Eclipse (if desired), and provide a few additional resources.

Zend understands that many additional libraries exist within the Eclipse environs, and that is one of the main reasons the company has developed Zend Studio for Eclipse—to leverage off the many Eclipse add-on tools.

Zend Studio for Eclipse Update Process

Before you install new add-on libraries, however, you need to know that your installation of Zend Studio for Eclipse is up-to-date. From time to time, you should verify that you have the latest release in case you miss an announcement from Zend.

Under the Help menu in Zend Studio for Eclipse is an item called Software Updates. Clicking on this item gives you two options: Find and Install (discussed in the next section) and Manage Configuration. Clicking on this second item brings up a window similar to that shown in Figure A.1.

Here, you can see all the features that you currently have installed, and if necessary, you can verify individual installed components for their updates. Better yet, if you have the time, click on the top level of the tree view and then click on Scan for Updates in the right panel. By doing so, you scan the Web for any updates available for every component that you have installed. We said "If you have the time…" because this is indeed a lengthy process, so be sure to have a few other things to do while you're waiting for this process to complete.

When the search for updates is completed, you are presented with a selection window for all (if any) updates that were located on the Web. You can then select only the updates you want or all of them and begin the update process. Some of the updates may ask you to consent to licensing agreements before you can update, but that is just a formality.

The update process is quite straightforward and really very easy to follow.

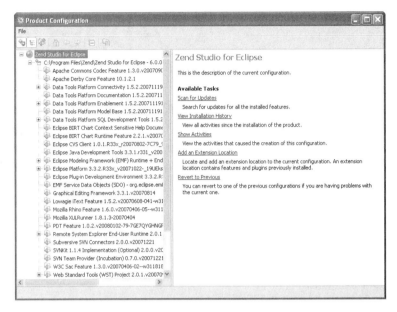

Figure A.1   Zend Studio for Eclipse Product Configuration window.

Adding Third-Party Plug-ins to Zend Studio for Eclipse

Adding new plug-ins to the Zend Studio for Eclipse environment is a little different process. For starters, it would really help you to know just what kind of plug-in you are after and where you can obtain it on the Web. We strongly suggest that you spend the time up front looking at the plethora of plug-ins available and make sure you get the one that you want. It's not that uninstalling a plug-in is difficult, but you would be potentially wasting a lot of time.

Check out the downloads page at Eclipse.org for a listing of available plug-ins and do the research into the ones that you really want:

    http://www.eclipse.org/downloads/index_topic.php

This site provides a listing of all the Eclipse downloads available arranged in order of topic.

We have chosen to install a graphics design plug-in as an example because it is visually easy to verify that it was installed properly. The plug-in is called the Graphical Modeling Framework (GMF), and you can read all about it at Eclipse.org:

    http://www.eclipse.org/gmf/

You will notice that many of these plug-ins have their own subhome page on the Eclipse web space. Be sure to read the FAQ file and summary of what any particular plug-in will do so that you are familiar with any issues about it.

Installing the Library

Now let's start the process of obtaining and installing a plug-in. Regaining your focus in Zend Studio for Eclipse, if you select Help, Software Updates, Find and Install, you are asked to search for current installation updates or search for new features to install. Select the New Features option, and the window shown in Figure A.2 opens.

Figure A.2   New plug-in install process with the Europa site selected.

Note

The tricky part about the installation process is knowing which update site possess the plug-in that you desire. This one (GMF) happens to be in the Europa Site, but that information is not very easy to find on the GMF site (see Figure A.3). We found it in the setup guide of the tutorial on the company's Wiki pages, so be sure to look for information there. You may also find this information in a FAQ entry. You may also notice that the Product name listed in the install process does not totally match that shown on its Eclipse site, as is true in this case.

After you locate and select the appropriate plug-in and finish the wizard process, click on the Install button to start the download and actually install the add-on. Figure A.4 shows the process with the status bars underway during the install.

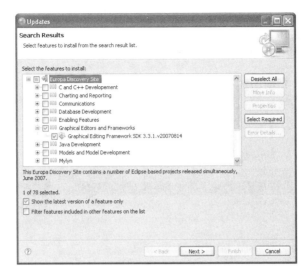

Figure A.3   Plug-in install process with GMF plug-in selected.

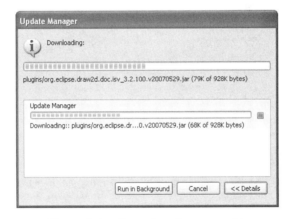

Figure A.4   Plug-in install process with
GMF being downloaded and set up.

CAUTION

Some plugins are acquired in a multi-step process where you have to install an SDK (Software Development Kit) collection before you can install and use the plugin. If this is the case, simply select Find and Install from the Software Updates menu under Help and follow that install process again. It helps if you install the SDK first. Be sure to follow any installation instructions that you can find on the plug-ins specific web sites.

Depending on the plug-in that you pick, you may either have to apply the updates or restart Zend Studio for Eclipse for the new software to become active.

Ensuring the Plug-in Works

Be sure to read the documentation for the particular plug-in you choose. In this case we can simply open one of the sample projects (File, New, Example menu path) that came with the plug-in and start from there. It shows that the plug-in was installed correctly and is working fine. Figure A.5 shows one of the samples that came with the plug-in that we chose.

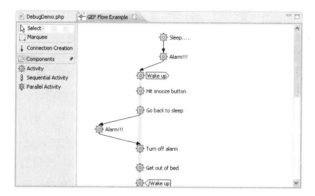

Figure A.5   GMF plug-in in action.

> **Note**
>
> When you have your environment in place, there is even a way to ensure that your IDE is always up-to-date: scheduling an automatic update. Under the Preferences area of the Window menu, you can select Install/Update and then Automatic Updates to schedule your update process for as often as you like. This is a great feature to give you peace of mind about your IDE environment being current.

Additional Resources

We could not address many areas within the Eclipse world in this book. In an attempt to provide some of the connections available, we've included the following list, which shows some of the additional resources that are accessible and the means to obtaining them.

> **Note**
>
> The provided URLs are accurate at the time this book was published; they may change at any time.

- http://www.zend.com/en/products/studio/
  Home page for the Studio for Eclipse professional version.
- http://www.zend.com
  Zend home page: The place to get the latest information about Zend and its respective products.
- www.eclipse.org
  Eclipse Foundation home page: The web location to get information on all things Eclipse, including both base and plug-in releases and upgrades.
- http://www.pearsoned.com/professional/index.htm
  Pearson Education home page: The web location for the publisher of this title and countless other technical titles.
- http://devzone.zend.com/public/view
  Zend Developer Zone: Discussion forums, tutorials, articles, news, and events related to all of Zend's products.
- http://framework.zend.com/
  Zend Framework home page: The site for discussions on the Framework library that is used in the project within this book.
- http://www.eclipse.org/pdt/index.php
  Eclipse PDT project page: The web location for the PHP Development Tools open source "light" version on Zend Studio for Eclipse.
- http://eclipse.sys-con.com/
  Eclipse Developer's Journal: The website for all things related to Eclipse and its many veins.
- http://www.php.net/
  PHP's home page: The place to get the latest news and downloads of the web programming language PHP.
- http://www.paladin-bs.com/
  Peter MacIntyre's website.
- http://www.geckoware.com/
  Ian Morse's website.

Index

T

W

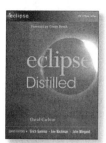

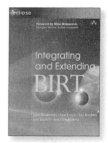

REGISTER THIS BOOK

Register this book and unlock benefits exclusive to the owners of this book.

Registration benefits can include

- Additional content
- Book errata
- Source code, example files, and other downloads
- Increased membership discounts
- Discount coupons
- A chance to sign up to receive content updates, information on new editions, and more

Book registration is free and takes only a few easy steps:

1. Go to **www.informit.com/register**
2. Enter the book's ISBN
   (found above the barcode on the back of your book).
3. You will be prompted to either register for or log in to informit.com.
4. Once you have completed your registration or log in, you will be taken to your "My Registered Books" page.
5. This page will list any benefits associated with each title you register, including links to content and coupon codes.

The benefits of book registration vary with each book, so be sure to register every Pearson Technology Group book you own to see what else you might unlock at **www.informit.com/register**

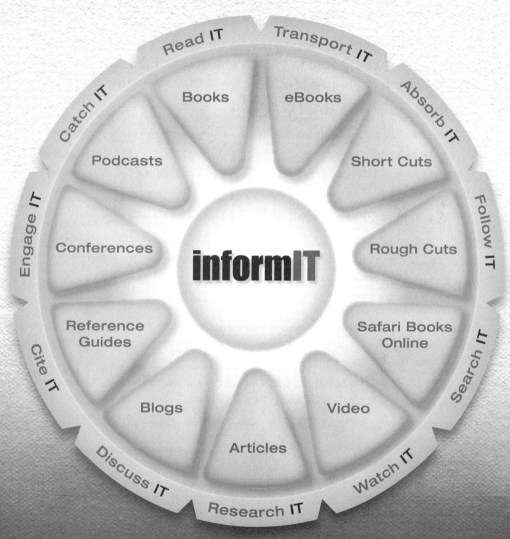